AYYA KHEMA

COME AND SEE FOR YOURSELF

The Buddhist Path to Happiness

WINDHORSE PUBLICATIONS

Also by Ayya Khema:

Be An Island
Being Nobody, Going Nowhere
I Give You My Life
Visible Here and Now
When the Iron Eagle Flies
Who Is My Self?

Published by Windhorse Publications
11 Park Road
Birmingham
B13 8AB

Original German edition © Jhana Verlag 1998
English translation © Windhorse Publications 2002

Cover design Marlene Eltschig
Cover photo of Ayya Khema courtesy of Buddha-Haus
Printed by Biddles Ltd, Guildford, Surrey

ISBN 1 899579 45 1

Thanks are due to the following for their invaluable assistance:
Sanghamitta of Buddha-Haus, Stephanie Hammer of Jhana Verlag,
Michael Etzold, Punyamati, Jayachitta, and Vassika.

CONTENTS

About the Author

Ayya Khema was born of Jewish parentage in Berlin in 1923. She escaped from Germany to Scotland with 200 other children in 1938, and was eventually reunited with her parents in China. With the outbreak of the Second World War, she and her family were placed in a Japanese prisoner-of-war camp. After the war she emigrated to America and married. In the early 1960s she travelled extensively in Asia, and after ten years of meditation practice, she taught meditation and Buddhism in Europe, North America, and Australia.

Ayya Khema has been instrumental in the revitalization of women's monasticism in Buddhism. She was ordained in 1979 into the Theravāda tradition in Sri Lanka. Here she started the International Buddhist Women's Centre and Parappuduwa Nuns' Island for women. In 1987 she co-ordinated the first international conference of Buddhist nuns, which resulted in the creation of Sakyadhita, a world-wide Buddhist women's organization.

She has written over twenty books on meditation and Buddhism in English and German, and her most popular works include *Being Nobody, Going Nowhere*, which was awarded the Christmas Humphreys Memorial Award. Her work is characterized by a deep understanding of the practice and benefits of meditation and a call to simplify our daily lives and clarify our hearts and minds using the teachings of the Buddha.

In addition to establishing Wat Buddha Dhamma in Australia, a forest monastery in the Theravāda tradition, she was the spiritual director of Buddha-Haus in Germany, where she died in 1997.

Preface

Ayya Khema was born Jewish but ended her life as a Buddhist. She spent much of her life travelling around the world with her family, returning to Germany only late in life. Some of her adventures are described in her fascinating autobiography, *I Give You My Life*.

The first time I saw her was in a television documentary about a Buddhist community in Uttenbuehl, at the foot of the Bavarian Alps in southern Germany. The programme touched me, and some years later I was delighted to be able to help translate one of her books.

By that time I had moved to England, and I had reached a time in my life when I was finding it difficult to concentrate. For me this book was like a foundation course in Buddhism, being based on talks that Ayya Khema gave at the so-called open Wednesdays at Buddha-Haus in Uttenbuehl and first published in 1994. I particularly liked the fact that they are based on traditional Buddhist scriptures. Ayya Khema would recite some verses from the *Dhammapada* or some other short sūtra or text, and then comment and elaborate on it. She was happy to elucidate on the text to anyone interested in meditation and the teaching of the Buddha. By all accounts, including her own, Ayya Khema was herself committed to a strong meditation practice and she talked inspiringly about it. Indeed, her main emphasis was on how to incorporate our meditation practice into our daily lives.

Ayya Khema had no qualms about talking to her Christian 'colleagues', comparing her dhyanic meditative experiences with the *unio mystica* of people like Eckhart of Cologne (Meister Eckhart), and she would teach meditation and lead retreats in monasteries.

It was Dhammaloka who initially suggested that Windhorse Publications translate *Komm und sieh slebst (Come and See for Yourself)*, which was originally publised in 1994, into English. Jayachitta began the work of translation, and I carried it on. Jinananda then edited the text and Punyamati painstakingly checked the final draft. Sincere thanks go to all of them for their work. Portia Howe and the rest of the team at Windhorse Publications also put in a lot of work. Many other people have contributed in various ways, especially Sanghamitta from Buddha-Haus, Ulrike Harris, Asanga, Vassika, Ratnaprabha, Shantiprabha, and my partner Martina.

I would like to dedicate the translation of this book to all Buddhists in the West, and hope that all readers will catch a glimpse of the warm light that shines through the Buddha.

Michael Etzold
Oxford
December 2001

Whenever in the mind you contemplate
The groups of existence, how they arise and cease to be,
Rapture and happiness you will attain:
The one who knows calls it the deathless realm.

Dhammapada, stanza 374

1

Insight into Impermanence Leads to Happiness

THE PĀLI WORD *Dhammapada* may be translated 'Steps on the Path of the Teaching'. The celebrated work that goes by this name is divided into sections, each comprising a number of stanzas: groups of verses uttered by the Buddha on various occasions, each covering a different aspect of the teaching. However, the teaching is so concentrated that each stanza is in itself a little discourse.

In order to interpret the verse quoted opposite, I would like first to look at what some of the words really mean. The Buddha talks about our being able to attain rapture and happiness, and that is what we would all like to experience. Human beings search for happiness in many different ways and try to find it in many different things, usually external objects. We try, by whatever means, to acquire happiness, and once we have found it we want to keep it. We think we will always be happy if we can only hold on to that something or someone or event that once made us happy. So usually we try to find happiness in material things or in doing something that we think will satisfy us. But ever since life began, no one has managed to be happy all the time.

The Buddha is saying that in order to find happiness we have to practise. We may say that the work we do makes us feel happy, but however much we try to convince ourselves that we are satisfied because we are doing something useful, we find, when we look more closely, that this happiness does not last, and inwardly we remain restless and unstable. When people get depressed in this way they usually believe something external is wrong – they don't realize that what they experience is coming from within themselves.

Our ordinary thinking is concerned with wanting something. Even if what we want is skilful and wholesome, we find that – try as we may – we cannot be constantly happy, so then we want something new, something different. The Buddha offers us a completely fresh approach. He wants to teach us new ways of thinking, to show us a way of switching to another level: one based on reality rather than wishing. For example, if we have already tried everything and realized that material things do not make us happy, there is already some happiness in that insight alone. In our text the Buddha says:

> *Whenever in the mind you contemplate*
> *The groups of existence, how they arise and cease to be,...*

These 'groups (or heaps) of all existence' are the components of our being. First, there is our body, with which we identify, thinking 'This is me.' Then there is the mind, of which the Buddha has distinguished four aspects: First, sense consciousness – which we experience initially through being in contact with our senses of sight, hearing, smell, taste, or touch; secondly, feeling, either pleasant or unpleasant, which arises on the basis of sense contact, and includes the emotions; thirdly, the perception that follows upon feeling; fourthly, the reactions to our perception of the contact – also referred to as mental formations.

We could break the mind down even further, to include, for example, the will as one of its components. However, we usually focus on just these four: sense contact, feeling, perception, and reaction.

It is worth trying to bear in mind these five groups of existence, or at least the division into body and mind, the other four being the means by which we can address the question of what the mind really is. You can check out this process right now: at this very moment your experience includes seeing, touching, and possibly hearing. You may not be smelling or tasting anything just now, but three of your senses are certainly making contact. In doing so, they produce a residue of feeling, which we might not notice if we didn't deliberately practise awareness. The original feeling is often very subtle, and we get caught up in the subsequent reaction instead, which is much stronger. Between these, however, comes perception, and this too is an individual matter. Though two people see the same object, each perceives something different and reacts accordingly; whereas one person sees something beautiful, the other may be indifferent to it, or even find it ugly. This is why we hardly notice feeling and perception. If we hear someone say something we might think to ourselves 'that's nonsense,' or 'that's great,' or 'I'm not interested,' or 'I already know that.' We are so continually absorbed in our reactions that it is hard to realize that between sense contact and reaction there are also feeling and perception. As a first step, therefore, we should investigate our sense contacts and the resultant reactions. These are not difficult to recognize, and the process will help us to become familiar with the groups of existence.

We generally respond to our reactions and aim to improve on them by somehow modifying our sense contacts. We aim to see, hear, taste, smell, or touch something different, but we are always guided by old modes of thought. You'd think we'd soon have had enough of this strategy, and exhausted its possibilities, but in fact we are only too willing to keep taking up the endless opportunities we are given to see, hear, smell, taste, or touch something new. However, there is an alternative to following the same old track: we can strike out on a new path, one that consists in observing our reactions instead of identifying with them.

This is easier said than done. It is something we definitely need to practise, since we all proceed on the assumption that we should identify with our reactions, which are right and proper ones. They are, after all, *our* reactions. If we consider reactions, even negative ones, to be justified simply because they are *our* reactions, then it is only natural that we will continue to expect happiness to come from outside ourselves. Consequently, we avoid things that cause unpleasant reactions, and we keep searching for whatever we think will bring us pleasure. Of course, try as we may, we have no hope of experiencing a lifetime of entirely pleasurable sense contacts, but this does not stop us from being so totally absorbed in this objective that we are oblivious to the possibility of an entirely different route. Even without actively looking for them, we will experience pleasant sense contacts. One benefit of living on the human plane of existence is that there is no shortage of them. Most of us have tasty things to eat and drink, enjoyable weather, the blossoming of flowers, and the pleasure of conversation. There is no harm in these, but if we place our trust in our reactions, and give ourselves over to the search for pleasant experiences, we will be disappointed again and again. We will never find inner happiness via that route. It is for this reason that in the above stanza the Buddha instructs us to contemplate how the groups of existence arise and cease, how they come and go. And the way to do this is simply to pay attention to ourselves. Busy as we are with scrutinizing others, it does not occur to us that before we can really get to know someone we have to see into ourselves. What we recognize in others is only what we have already discovered within ourselves.

One should be able to observe the arising and cessation of thoughts and feelings, their coming and going, quite clearly and distinctly; this is really not difficult. Yet we are so engrossed in the content of our reactions that we don't notice how quickly they vanish. A thought usually disappears almost as soon as it arises, except in so far as a new one is based upon it in the course of a train of thought – and even then the initial thought has disappeared. No doubt we could have written it down as it arose, but it might be of no interest to us later because the flow of thoughts is constantly changing.

Most people don't like to confront the fact that their thoughts and feelings are impermanent. Once this is brought to their notice, however, very few can resist the force of this truth, because we all carry proof of it within ourselves. Such transitoriness challenges our perception of the self, making it seem less concrete and sure of its ground, and this brings us up against our big problem, which is that we see ourselves as solid and substantial, set and fixed into what we call a person, with views, opinions, and identities that make up our 'ego'. Our view of ourselves, and the assurance of our ego, is shaken when we realize that those views and opinions, thoughts and feelings, are in fact constantly coming and going.

The less firmly established our ego, the easier it is to be happy. We don't have simply to assent to this equation, nor is there any excuse to reject it out of hand, for we may investigate it for ourselves. The more we want to assert ourselves and hold our own, to 'be someone' with a certain set of views, a personalized belief system, and a privileged identity, the more we have to cling to all these things that make us who we are, and try to make it all solid. However, since things are constantly arising and ceasing, we are confronted by an impossible task. This is why human beings are not happy.

We are all in the same predicament. As long as we try to assert ourselves and hold on to other people or the things with which we identify, we cannot be free and happy. Instead – whether we are busy or whether we do nothing at all – we will feel constantly under pressure, what nowadays we call stressed. In fact, this pressure under which human beings put themselves has always been there, because it reinforces our sense of identity and the need to assert ourselves that produces it in the first place. We like to tell ourselves that we are solid and substantial beings with clearly defined characteristics, so we say things like 'I'm sorry I'm late, but that's how I am,' or 'I have to cry when movies are sad – that's just me.'

Statements like these are nonsense, because no form or quality is unchangeable. Every thought, every feeling, comes and goes. We need only to consider for a moment whether the feelings or thoughts we had today are still there. When we look, that thought of a moment ago has already disappeared. Indeed, there is nothing – not even our own life – that we can hold on to. Although we grow older all the time, some people cannot deal with this fact. Even worse, they are not even aware they cannot deal with it. We hold on to our memories in such a way that we do not notice ourselves growing older, and all these memories make up an apparent self. In this way we build up an even more confirmed sense of self.

Evidence that contradicts our notion of the way things are can be found everywhere. Take the weather, for example. Suppose it's raining: each drop of rain falls to the ground and dissolves; it seeps into the earth and is gone. And we do the same. We are just like the raindrops, but we prefer to ignore the law of birth and death.

There is no compulsion to believe what the Buddha promised, but surely we can meet him halfway and agree to investigate the truth of this law. Bearing it constantly in mind in order to fully understand it and attain bliss and happiness is a big undertaking. We can experience bliss in meditation, but the inner happiness that every human being tries to find arises through insight. Insight can evolve in a meditative and mindful life, but even meditation is impermanent: as soon as we get up from our meditation, the pleasant meditative state has gone.

Even before he was Enlightened, the Buddha was a very good meditator. He was familiar with the eight absorptions, and through them he experienced rapture, bliss, tranquillity, and infinity.

However, after these great experiences he grew dissatisfied again, because he longed for them to be repeated. Therefore he wanted to stabilize his insight in such a way that external conditions would no longer perturb him. To put it briefly, the spiritual path means the consolidation of our inner happiness to such an extent that it becomes independent and is no longer unsettled by external circumstances.

There is a long way to go. But even the longest journey starts with a single step. Many steps have to be made, but the decisive one is the first, consisting in this exercise of the mind reflecting on impermanence. It is not only the impermanence of material things that we have to consider. (In a wealthy society such as ours, nobody is bothered about that anyway; as soon as something is broken, we just replace it.) We have to think of ourselves as impermanent, too. We may do this by taking the groups of existence – the body, sense contacts, feelings, perceptions, and reactions – and examining their impermanence. We should clearly recognize our dependence on external sense impressions – that hearing something we do not like can irritate us for the rest of the day, or that in not getting what we want we feel disappointed. There is no human being who would not prefer to avoid all this unpleasantness, but trying to hear only what we want to hear, to see only what we want to see, and to get only what we want to have, is an absurd way to go about it: it is a hopeless enterprise. The only reasonable way to examine this problem and deal with it is to consider and realize the true impermanence of everything.

We can all remember our childhood and some of the events from that period. It may not even seem that long ago. Yet how many things have happened since? And why do we now react quite differently from the way we did then? We like to think we are the same person, yet nothing in us remains as it was. All our feelings and thoughts have altered in character, along with the more obvious physical changes. Even if some vestige of the way we were remains, what made us who we were then is entirely different from what makes us who we are now.

This transformation is actually taking place from one day to the next – from one *second* to the next, to be precise. We cannot hold on to any of our experiences, and as long as we try to hold on to situations or people it is guaranteed that we will be disappointed because the endeavour is impossible. The plain and certain truth is that we cannot hold on to either our lives or our thoughts or our feelings; sense contacts, too, change from moment to moment. We have a certain success in preserving a simulacrum of our thoughts in the form of books and tapes – but those are not the original thoughts. You can look at your life right now, and see how it is passing by. If you know where to look it is not difficult to apply the mind to this task. Observing how your life unfolds, you can see that it is in constant flux.

As human beings, we do not like this sliding and disintegration, so we build up habits: we make a point of doing the same things at the same time every day. The more habits we get into the more we get some sense of fixity, of something solid, and with that, the promise of security in regular repetition. However, this is a very precarious assumption, for a habit is just a habit, which is nowhere near something that could constitute a solid and self-sustaining 'I'. We are continually searching for this sense of something solid to fit neatly into the framework we have set out in our habits. Yet whatever we do find within such a fixed framework, there is no chance of finding the kind of happiness we are really looking for, which is inner happiness that is independent of external circumstances.

External factors are largely beyond our control. All too often they descend on us without the opportunity to do anything about them. We do not like to accept this unpalatable truth, however. We should like to retain control over our lives, as well as experience inner happiness, independently of external circumstances, but this is hopeless. We are in the same situation as 'Hans in Luck' in Grimm's fairy tale of that name, who is rewarded for many years of service to his master with a precious lump of gold, and on the way home to his mother exchanges the gold for other more or less useful things, finally arriving with another lump in his pocket: a worthless stone. Finally, he drops the stone and enjoys a great sense of relief. Exactly the same happens on our spiritual journey. In the search for something that does not exist, the only solution is to drop what we are carrying around with us. The stone we carry around with us, the burden on our shoulders, is ego-assertion, our identification with what appears solid and fixed, and which we call 'ego' or 'self', the apparent rootedness of our actions and thoughts in something solid and coherent. But how long-lasting are our accomplishments? They exist only in the distant past. We now live only with the results of those actions. Things can only come and go – nothing in our experience endures.

This whole world, even the whole universe, can never fulfil our deepest desire. Fulfilment does not come from anything out there – it comes from within. This is where the spiritual life differs essentially from the worldly life: it takes place within ourselves. And when we stop searching for happiness in the world and look to the depths of meditation instead, we discover that we carry within ourselves everything for which we have been searching. We just need to learn how to concentrate the mind – which is not as difficult as we might think – and we have the means to contact our inner life at any time. It is a matter of simply sitting down and practising every day. Just as we feed our body every day, we need to minister to the health of our mind. No one is going to question the necessity to feed the body, but it should also be pointed out that we need to take equally good care of our mind. During meditation the mind ceases to pay attention to what is happening in the world. It becomes absorbed in itself and, as a result, aspects of our experience already present in rudimentary form have the chance to emerge. First, we may experience rapture, the factor that distinguishes the first absorption. This pleasant sensation is available to everyone, but it is normally obscured by thought, hence the need to suspend thought by concentrating the mind in meditation. If we maintain this practice, it will one day become clear to us that the mind can stop its chatter.

Once we have gained access to our inner life by this means, once we have experienced this first stage, we will know for certain that this inner world is not to be found in the outer world, but in meditation. We will know for sure that there is a way that leads us to what we have always searched for, and what the world cannot give us. From this point on, we will be happy to be absorbed not in our own reactions to things, as they ceaselessly come and go, but in the coming and going itself.

Broadly speaking, as human beings we are all the time totally absorbed in our reactions to things, and we search the world for that perfect situation in which those reactions are going to be as pleasant as possible. But once we have experienced rapture in meditation, this search for pleasant experiences is not so all-consuming, for we know implicitly that we have only to turn inwards and we will find all we would otherwise have expected from the world. We are then also willing to focus on the coming and going itself, instead of on our reactions to what is coming and going.

When we begin this practice, we keep losing our awareness of impermanence; everything else seems so much more important, and things remain much the same. It takes an effort to understand properly the impermanent nature of everything. It may take some encouragement to persuade the mind to accept this principle not only intellectually – on this level we are probably able to appreciate it well enough – but also emotionally. Suddenly, however, we find ourselves seeing things as things that fade away.

When we have actually felt that everything is in continuous flux, our resistance to that truth ceases. When we see things as they are, that they change anyway, we no longer try to wish them other than they are. We also lose that sense of recoiling from whatever we dislike or do not want to experience, and the corresponding sense of regret or craving for whatever we should like to experience. In that moment, when our inner aversion ceases, we halt the search for happiness, and clearly recognize that we are already in possession of the treasure we sought.

In many cultures there are stories about someone setting out in search of a pot of gold, looking everywhere for the right spot to dig. Finally some wise person tells them – and this is a version from the Jewish tradition – 'Go home, the treasure is under your kitchen table.' So they return home and start digging under the kitchen table until it suddenly dawns on them: 'The treasure is within myself, not under the kitchen table! I just have to put my feet under the kitchen table.' We search and search, while all the time we carry the grail within ourselves.

This is of course something we have to find out for ourselves. It is not enough just to decide we want to discover these inner riches; we have to do something about it. If we simply carry on as before and don't make any effort, we will continue to rely on the person we have always been, and to identify with our transient reactions to the world.

What the Buddha promises is that if we can achieve a sufficiently clear and deep recognition of the coming and going of the heaps of existence, we will be able to see ourselves in the same way – as a continuous interlocking of cause and effect. If we understand ourselves as cause and effect, ego-assertion will cease, for we are both cause and effect and both have their origins in our ongoing assertion of our egos.

If, in meditation, we get a clear sense of this coming and going, from moment to moment, and keep returning, again and again, even now, to the contemplation of impermanence, we will enter the deathless realm. This is the Buddha's promise.

The last line of the verse reads, 'The one who knows calls it the deathless realm.' Instead of 'one who knows' we could say, 'wise one'. It is not enough, after all, just to know something; we have to able to do it, or put it into practice. Knowing about something and being able to do it are not the same thing at all. To say that everything is impermanent is no great revelation – *knowing* impermanence is not the problem for us. But *being able to* requires the wisdom of being there – of really *being* what we *know*. This is the main difference between a scholar and a meditator. The scholar knows everything about impermanence, but only the meditator will one day be able to realize it. 'The one who knows' is therefore the wise one, and what the wise one knows is the 'deathless realm', a synonym for *nibbāna*.

Nibbāna is a difficult idea to understand, and one about which we can never say anything very precise. We might, for example, take it to mean the realization of 'god' within ourselves – not a god in any shape or form, but as the fundamental basis of everything that exists. That, we may say, is nibbāna. Unfortunately, the meanings of the word 'god' are so complex that it doesn't carry the right associations for most people, if it has any meaning at all any more; similarly there is also much confusion about the word 'nibbāna'.

Ideally, we should avoid forming any conceptual associations with regard to the word 'nibbāna'. However, I will give some indication of its meaning in order to point in the direction of what is really meant by the expression, 'deathless realm'. 'Deathless' means that nothing passes away – but nothing passes away only if nothing arises. At the very basis of all existence there is neither life nor death.

In order to realize this truth, we have to approach it very gradually. It has nothing to do with belief in an external reality, or with external rituals or external effects on us. If we are fortunate enough to live somewhere pleasant, to have enough food, to be protected from the severities of the weather, and to have medicine when we are ill, we have all we need from the outside world. We can all realize the highest truth because we carry it within ourselves. Subconsciously we know that this is what we are searching for, but people never talk about it openly, and do not want to admit it even to themselves. This truth does not necessarily have to have a name, be it nibbāna or the deathless realm, nor does it need to be called god. There is a reality in which we can find rest, but we can find it only within ourselves. There is also a voice that gives us advice, and it too comes from within. Yet we still keep searching in the wrong direction.

What is this state of rest? Is it retirement? Most people who have retired do not rest. They are often busier than ever, otherwise they would feel bored. Worldly rest only changes the things with which we are occupied. Finding rest is finding the existential basis of ourselves, the ground of our being, and realizing it. This basis is present in all of us. It has brought us to life, it keeps us alive, and it brings us death. Realizing it means letting go of the grasping and craving for being, and for being 'someone'. Therefore, only when we cease to grasp and crave for existence and ego validation can we truly find rest. This is not to say we should belittle or repudiate ourselves – which would be just as bad as egoistic craving. Rather, with the help of meditation we should come to realize how creation has come about within us.

As soon as we are able to stop our thinking, we have the opportunity to experience a new layer of our inner life – which is to say that this inner life we seek is an experience, not a thought process. The suspension of thought is the first step, showing us where to find deeper truth. At the same time we may prepare for that experience by directing our thoughts towards the fact that everything that happens to us and around us is impermanent. By persistently reminding ourselves of that, we may actually come to experience how everything comes and goes.

To remember what we know is simple. Mastery, on the other hand, is to experience what we know, and this is not as simple – though there are always some people in this world who have this mastery. We need not devote ourselves to a particular faith, religion, philosophy, or psychology; we need simply to keep an eye on ourselves. What could be simpler? But it is deceptively so. In fact, it is very difficult. What could be more interesting than keeping an eye on the self? But most people like to keep an eye on others. If we think of what we are taking in being like a movie, keeping an eye on ourselves definitely makes a movie that is a bit more worth watching than just keeping the camera rolling on external events without that awareness.

So we have the Buddha's promise that we can find inner happiness, independent of all external conditions. We also have our own guidelines for the path we must follow in order to experience it for ourselves. The tremendous usefulness and importance of the teaching of the Buddha is not just in its promise, but in showing us how we can realize the truth and what we can expect along the way.

Thus have I heard. Once the Exalted One was staying at Sāvatthi, in the Jeta Grove, in Anāthapiṇḍika's monastery. Late one night, a deity appeared to the Exalted One and, illuminating the entire Jeta grove with its radiant beauty, bowed to him respectfully and stood to one side. Standing thus, the deity addressed the Exalted One: 'Many gods and humans, in search of happiness, have reflected upon that which brings salvation. Oh you, may you now proclaim supreme salvation!'

Not associating with fools. Keeping the company of wise ones. Paying reverence to those who are worthy of reverence. These are great blessings.

Having one's abode in a favourable place, gaining merit in the past, and the pursuit of higher aspirations: these, truly, are great blessings!

Being rich in knowledge and skill, the moral precepts well practised, and using only well-spoken words. These, truly, are great blessings!…

Self-surrender and purification, insight into the noble truths, finally Enlightenment itself, these truly are great blessings!

A heart not trembling – sorrowless, stainless, and secure – even when touched by the eight worldly phenomena. This is a great blessing.

Those who attain that are invincible at all times and all places. They find happiness everywhere, and this is the supreme blessing.

Mahāmaṅgala Sutta, Sutta-Nipāta 258–69

2

The Thirty-Eight Blessings

IN THIS DISCOURSE, the Buddha explains what constitute the true blessings of humanity. This teaching is especially interesting because it is concerned with our day-to-day life. It begins as follows:

> *Thus have I heard. Once the Exalted One was staying at Sāvatthi, in the Jeta Grove, in Anāthapiṇḍika's monastery. Late one night, a deity appeared to the Exalted One and, illuminating the entire Jeta grove with its radiant beauty, bowed to him respectfully and stood to one side. Standing thus, the deity addressed the Exalted One: 'Many gods and humans, in search of happiness, have reflected upon that which brings salvation. Oh you, may you now proclaim supreme salvation!'*

We can imagine this deity either as a vision in the mind of the Buddha, or an external manifestation such as we might term an apparition, which we are perhaps familiar with in the Christian heritage in the form of the Virgin Mary or some other religious figure. But this deity speaks; it says that many gods and humans looking for happiness have been reflecting about that which brings salvation. No doubt we all have thought in one way or another about what would make us supremely happy. So what does the deity mean by salvation?

In asking the Buddha what he thinks about salvation, he is using the term in the sense of external events, magic symbols, and lucky charms. We, too, are often inclined to seek our happiness using tarot cards, astrology, numerology, and so on. But the Pāli word *maṅgala* has two meanings: it can be used as the deity uses it here, to mean 'salvation', but it can also mean 'blessing'. Here, as so very often, the Buddha does not take up the definition implied in the question; instead he sets out to explain of what true blessings consist, and describes a series of thirty-eight blessings that we can all acquire by our own efforts.

This vision appears to the Buddha in the monastery donated to him by a very rich man called Anāthapiṇḍika, where the Buddha often spent the three months of the rainy-season retreat. But although the vision is of unimaginable beauty, although it radiates purity and illuminates the entire grove, it has nothing to teach the Buddha. Rather, the Buddha is asked to explain the truth to the deity. He explains the first three blessings as follows:

> *Not associating with fools. Keeping the company of wise ones. Paying reverence to those who are worthy of reverence. These are great blessings.*

The first two blessings are related, and make a point about who we should spend time with: those from whose wisdom we may benefit. We cannot always choose those we come into contact with in our daily life; while earning our living we may have to make the best of those with whom we're thrown together. But, fortunately, we have quite a lot of spare time nowadays to spend as we like.

There are sayings like 'birds of a feather flock together' and 'you may know someone by the company he keeps', that remind us of this principle – enunciated by the Buddha in many discourses – about the great blessing of good friends, and the bane of mixing with the foolish and unwise. But how do we know who are the fools? According to the Buddha, these are people who have no interest in the spiritual life and who believe they can find happiness in material things. Most people will agree that true happiness cannot be found in material things alone. Every religion expresses this truth – 'Man does not live by bread alone.'

A foolish or unwise person is one who believes that what we see with our eyes, what we hear with our ears, what we smell with our nose, what we taste with our tongue, what we touch with our body, and what we think with our mind, comprise everything there is. But this view severely limits our potential. The mind has far-reaching and profound capacities, and subliminally we are aware of these, otherwise we should certainly never dream of sitting down on a meditation cushion and taking the trouble to work at something that is supposed to bring about more elevated mental states. So if we rely only on our senses, or assume we can find happiness within the world, then the Buddha calls us fools. In order to be certain that we ourselves are not fools, we must ask ourselves if we make any effort to seek out the company of the wise.

The wise person is not one who has learned a lot and knows a lot, but one who dwells in a world of purity and beauty they have found within. Such are those whose company we should go and search for – people who can help us on a spiritual level.

The third blessing is 'paying reverence to those who are worthy of reverence'. This is somewhat difficult in Western society, because we have little understanding of who is really worthy of reverence. In Asia you still find many people to whom reverence is shown, mostly for reasons of tradition. In the West we tend to be much too sceptical. It may be just as bad to be guilty of the opposite – gullibility – but however uncritical it might be, it at least enables us to feel and show something from the heart. Reverence and love both come from the same place.

In those places where the religious and the spiritual are highly valued in society, reverence is often shown towards those who have entirely devoted themselves to the religious life, like monks, nuns, roshis, and lamas. Whether they have actually achieved a high level of perfection, we cannot, of course, know; we can only recognize in someone else what we have in ourselves. In a sense, what we see in another person mirrors those qualities in ourselves.

In order to cultivate positive emotional qualities we should not be afraid to show reverence, even if we are not sure whether the person in question is spiritually immaculate. Our inclination to analyse others can easily nullify any feelings of reverence. Indeed, the Buddha repeatedly recommends that we take ourselves rather than someone else as the object of our analysis, and offers us a variety of approaches and methods to this end.

Once we have accepted the Buddha as our teacher we pay reverence to him from the bottom of our heart, and demonstrate that reverence through bowing. We also accord him respect through our effort to call to mind as much of his teaching as we can, so that the purity of the Dhamma can unfold within us. Reverence gives us a sense of connection with the highest ideal, and this in turn brings us an inner contentment and satisfaction that no reward from the material world can equal. There are various names we can give to this highest ideal of Enlightenment, but we may say that its quintessence, whether or not we manage to realize it for ourselves, is the Buddha. If we can show our reverence for the ideal in this way, by revering those worthy of reverence, the Buddha calls this a true blessing.

> *Having one's abode in a favourable place, gaining merit in the past, and the pursuit of higher aspirations: these, truly, are great blessings!*

The first of these blessings is something of a very down-to-earth nature: a favourable environment, according to the Buddha, is a place without war or hostile neighbours. Where tranquillity prevails we can relax and have space for contemplation. If we live in such a place we can consider ourselves very lucky. The Buddha counts it among the thirty-eight blessings.

The next blessing, 'gaining merit in the past', is the blessing of having created good karma through love, readiness to help others, and generosity. It is so easy to forget that everything we think, say, and do brings results, that nothing gets lost. The effects of our intentions and actions may sometimes appear within a day, or even within a second, or they may come to fruition only after a very long time. Our life is our responsibility alone. To quote another saying, 'Life is what you make it.' We may well believe that it is external circumstances that make us happy or unhappy, but these circumstances depend in turn upon our intentions. Our happiness lies in our own hands. Good results derive from good actions; bad results flow from bad actions. This is the law of cause and effect.

Of course, it rarely works out quite as simply as that. If we have a good intention but lack the skill to put it into practice, we will gain some beneficial results and some not so beneficial ones. The Buddha said that the workings of karma in terms of cause and effect are like a spider's web: the threads are interwoven in such a way that one cannot find either the beginning or the end. In the same way we cannot find out exactly what has brought about our present conditions, or get to the bottom of why we are how we are. What we can do, however, is be grateful for the good things in our life every day. Gratitude lends the heart a positive, loving, appreciative, and affirmative quality, and in doing so supports our efforts to keep doing good.

Doing good starts in the mind with good thoughts, is expressed in skilful speech, and then manifests in the form of positive action. Our three gateways, therefore, are thought, word, and deed. It is through these gateways that every human being in the world brings about good and bad karma. If we have created good karma in the past, it is a great blessing that this good karma is now supporting us – and we can continue to protect ourselves from bad karma by being aware of thought, word, and deed. There is, after all, no one in this world who does not make any karma, except an Enlightened One.

The next blessing is 'the pursuit of higher aspirations'. This can also be translated as 'having a good direction in life'. Here again we come back to the fact that worldly things cannot satisfy anyone. If we observe our relatives, acquaintances, and friends, and if we take a good look at ourselves, too, it becomes crystal clear that life consists of a mixture of joy and grief, the pleasant and the unpleasant.

We like to think that whatever is unpleasant has been brought about by unsatisfactory external events, and consequently we work hard to change these circumstances. At some stage we notice that in spite of all this we are still not able to make everything right. For a start, many conditions we come up against simply cannot be altered. And yet, even after we have acknowledged this, we still reckon that exceptions to this experience can be found, and that once the external circumstances have been sorted out, everything will be sorted out. But the fact is that external circumstances are not the real problem. If we want to commit ourselves to the highest ideal and follow a spiritual path, we can begin by ceasing to blame unfavourable external circumstances.

The Buddha's path consists of meditation and inner purification, each of which depends on the other. If we neglect one or both, there is no stable balance to our spiritual life. To reach the highest goal, one has to follow both paths. Meditation enables us to contemplate what really goes on within us, and without such self-knowledge the purification of thoughts and emotions is impossible.

The development of tranquillity in meditation, by focusing the mind, transforms it into a valuable tool. The Buddha has compared this mind to a sharpened axe: we know for ourselves that for critical jobs a blunt instrument simply will not do; similarly, only a sharpened mind can learn the really important things in life.

We allow ourselves to be constantly disturbed and excited by trifles, although they serve no purpose other than to fill our days. Through meditation we can learn to distinguish between such outer values and true inner values. Of course, as long as we have a body we need to take care of the conditions in which we live. We have to sleep, eat, and work. But at the end of the day, how valuable are these activities in themselves? To what extent are they the means by which we manage to keep ourselves distracted in order to avoid noticing that we are unfulfilled?

There is an endless supply of distractions. In our high-tech society we only have to press a button in order to escape for a while. But what peace and happiness does that bring to our hearts and minds? The direction we want our lives to follow is a serious issue. How important are the things with which we busy ourselves, with which we occupy our minds, the things we pore over and spend time on? Is their value internal or external? Do they lead us and others to happiness and peace? These are the questions we have to ask ourselves if we are to lay down guidelines for bringing out the meaning of our lives.

> *Being rich in knowledge and skill, the moral precepts well practised, and using only well-spoken words. These, truly, are great blessings!*

The first of these next three blessings – 'being rich in knowledge and skill' – brings together two blessings that are vastly different from each other, practically speaking. Knowledge enriches our life tremendously, but can we put it into practice? We all know the counsel 'love your neighbour as yourself', but are we able and ready to follow that advice? These important questions have a claim to the careful consideration of every one of us.

At home, at school, or on training courses we have learned many skills that help us make a living. The Buddha especially emphasized craftsmanship because this enables us to be independent. It was highly valued in his day – much more so than today. We have neglected many of our skills, some surviving as little more than hobbies, and some we have even lost altogether, because today nearly everything is produced by machine, and if we want something we can just go out and buy it.

We often have skills we do not know about, because the opportunity to try them out has never arisen, yet it is a great blessing to be able to produce something with one's own hands. It helps us to become independent, whilst being able to please other people with what we make – with the possibility of creating right livelihood from our skill. The development and application of craft skills can help us to lead a more balanced life, and to become confident and valuable members of our community. However, the question in the end is to what extent we can actually 'realize' our knowledge and our skills so as to find inner peace – for a blessing must lead to peace, or it is not a blessing. If we believe that world peace depends on others working towards peace, then we need to take a fresh look at that belief. World peace depends on each of us finding peace within ourselves. This is the only road towards world peace.

The pairing of knowledge with skill is especially important for those students of the Buddha's teaching who are familiar with its content, and how it all fits together, but have problems translating it into practice. Intelligent people like us have no difficulty knowing something, understanding what we read, even learning it by heart. What we learned in school is still there, but how much of that is still alive within us after we have closed the book or finished the recitation? When the Buddha says 'knowledge *and* skill' he means that we should be concerned with both.

No doubt this discourse has significant secular applications, but its concern is with spiritual knowledge and the highest aspirations towards it. If we fail to take in – to internalize and pay heed to – the meaning of the words, the best knowledge will be useless. The Buddha described many cases of simple people who could remember merely one discourse, or just a single sentence of one, and still found the path to purification. He frequently observed that it was of no use merely to memorize a lot of words and speeches. Just one instruction pursued faithfully can be enough to lead us to happiness. Indeed, the *Mahāmaṅgala Sutta*, the discourse about great salvation, itself contains everything we need to guide our lives. The points it makes are not difficult to remember; it's just that everyday life so often distracts us: what we do seems so important that we can see no alternative, as if it were an absolute obligation.

Something that can help put things into perspective is the acknowledgement that we are all doomed to die. This has nothing to do with how old we are. The human lifespan varies considerably, but death is certain for every one of us. If we properly consider the fact of our own death we will not postpone so many things, saying as we often do, 'one day, when the kids are grown up, when my mortgage is paid off, when the weather is better,...'. There is no end to the things we can wait for. But we can only live now, in the present moment. Tomorrow is another day and we do not yet know whether we will live to see it. If we don't do today what we know we need to do, we will have wasted today.

The next blessing – 'the moral precepts well practised' – refers to the five precepts with which we have all been familiar in one form or another possibly since childhood. They are: not to kill, not to take what we have not been given, not to engage in sexual misconduct, not to lie or use coarse language, and not to take alcohol or other intoxicants.

Of course, it is much easier to learn these rules than to obey them. Abstention from killing includes not just humans, but all living beings, and we each need to consult our own conscience about this. As for not taking the not given, there is a positive corollary, to practise generosity. Likewise, not engaging in sexual misconduct is a matter not only of avoiding harming others, but also of fidelity: it is a question of being faithful to one's partner, as well as to other friends, and it includes upholding one's responsibilities to others, keeping solidarity with all that lives. The virtue of right speech is the subject of the next blessing, which we will discuss below. Since alcohol and other drugs confuse the mind even more, the Buddha recommends abstinence.

Observance of the moral precepts calls for a certain amount of self-discipline. These days, self-discipline is not as popular as it used to be. We take the view that first and foremost our lives should be comfortable, and our house and possessions are geared towards this end. But comfort is a relative value and it does not produce happiness. We need self-discipline if we are to gain a sense of true values in life or maintain a daily meditation practice. Self-discipline means giving up things that serve only to gratify our senses but do not in themselves have any higher value. This kind of self-discipline can be very demanding.

Not using coarse language concerns, obviously, our communication with other people. The positive counterpart to this precept tells us to use only well-spoken words. This does not mean saying what we think others would like to hear, which is part of the widespread bad habit of constantly fishing for praise. Well-spoken words are those concerned with the Dhamma, which have an inspiring and uplifting effect and which help people to adopt an orientation towards the good. Such words come from far deeper within ourselves than our everyday chat. The way the Buddha often recommends it to us, we should have 'noble' conversations with 'noble' friends.

Of course, even a noble conversation can express simple good will. Fundamentally, however, well-spoken words are those that heighten our awareness, that raise us above and beyond the individual and reveal the limited nature of the ego. They lead us to feel solidarity with all human beings and to realize the universal character of creation. In helping us to this sense of being part of the living unity of things, they can bring a feeling of safety – freedom from fear and anxiety. We cannot avoid discussion of everyday matters, but if we have no other kind of conversation – if we never engage with topics that reach towards a deeper truth than our illusory individuality – our life is impoverished.

The ground is prepared for such conversations by nourishing the mind through hearing, reading, and discussing the teachings. We should really take far more care with the way we feed the mind than with how we feed the body. Stimulation by television or newspapers is not usually beneficial, and we should not give them undue attention. There are many books and commentaries on the Buddha's teachings, offering fresh approaches to a higher consciousness, that we can better occupy ourselves with. The more we make a point of steeping ourselves in universal truths, the more naturally the mind will turn towards them.

We should make the most of the little time we have on earth, in this body, to realize our highest potential. We all have it within us to gain Enlightenment, that is, to achieve immaculate clarity and the end of all suffering and sorrow. But we have to take steps towards its realization, first of all by seeing that our everyday routine does nothing but keep us alive, and that since we are all going to die anyway, it can never be that important.

What we truly realize and work out within ourselves is something that does not depend on external things. Meditation is a tool to this end, necessary but not sufficient in itself. All the thirty-eight blessings in this discourse, starting with everyday benefits and taking us all the way to Enlightenment, are blessings we can achieve in this life, through our own efforts. The whole path shows us how best to use our abilities.

> *Supporting parents in every way, caring for the family, a peaceful and orderly occupation. These, truly, are great blessings!*

This means that wherever we give our best, we will find the supreme blessing, certainly for the time being. The experience of rich and rewarding states of mind is the product of a steady process of purifying our words and actions. With regard to support for parents, the blessing lies in our readiness to help, whether or not our parents ask for it, whether or not they need it, and whether or not we think they will be grateful. Helping our parents is always beneficial, whether we offer material, active, or emotional support. If we can also help with a pure heart it will always yield good results. It is good to perform good actions, but it is even better to accompany them with good thoughts: actions performed with mixed emotions bring unclear results, while unkind intentions definitely lead to more unkindness.

The Buddha often urged that we should be very grateful to our parents, because without them we should not be alive. They looked after us while we could not look after ourselves, and they did the best they could at the time. Nor should we ever forget that we chose them ourselves. To be kind and supportive later in life to those who were so helpful towards us in the beginning is good for us as well, in terms of creating positive karma.

'Caring for the family' is no doubt a familiar blessing to which to aspire. But many family conflicts seem to come down to something quite simple, which is that we have fixed ideas how things should be. In reality, nothing is how we dream it should be. Looking at human beings in general, and the nuclear family in particular, nothing is one hundred per cent perfect. Many people spend their whole lives searching for perfection on this human level, but it is a search for something that does not exist, and it results in disappointment and despair.

It is pointless to blame others or a particular set of circumstances. Nothing and nobody is responsible for the fact that the human level cannot be perfect. On the human plane of existence it is a great blessing if we can give without expecting results. Giving without seeking gratitude is something we can learn in the family. As soon as we look for a return, the spirit of generosity is tarnished by wanting something we feel is owed us, and not knowing whether we are going to get it. This in turn removes the joy of being open-handed.

Next, 'a peaceful and orderly occupation'. Mundane as it is, the way we make our living is an important spiritual issue. It should not harm or have any kind of negative effect on another being. It is worth checking whether we observe the five precepts in our work, so that we can enjoy this blessing. If we can find a job in which we can help others, so much the better.

Furthermore, our working life requires a certain stability – as well as a social dimension. Our time at work represents a considerable part of our lives and we need to observe the same rules for moral conduct here as in our private life. A peaceful and orderly occupation is also one in which we avoid getting over-excited or wound up by our work; one in which we avoid rivalry and the desire to earn a large amount of money. We should also avoid overwork – though it should also be said that some people become overworked very easily because, for one reason or another, they are not devoted to their work.

This blessing is not simply about our work as such. Peaceful and orderly conduct is vital to our meditation practice. If we do not meditate on a daily basis, are not fully committed to our practice, and to cap it all have problems at work, it will be difficult to follow this path. We can all reap the fruits of the blessings discussed here, but only if we incorporate them into our daily lives.

> *Generosity, right living, to make good karma – that, truly, is*
> *a great blessing!*

We have now reached a point in this discourse where it becomes clear that certain spiritual qualities are necessary that we do not find in a life driven by materialistic and economic concerns. The Buddha now gives a list of blessings that pertain to a more advanced level of the spiritual path. We are being asked to choose between the materialistic life and the truly spiritual life. Unfortunately, the difference between a life in which material values are given top priority and a life based on spiritual values is much easier to explain than to put into practice. In a materialistic life people want to get as much as they can, while in the spiritual life the idea is to *give* as much as possible. Everyone knows that to give is a greater blessing than to receive, but this is difficult to practise.

The next blessing on the list is generosity. Generosity has many different facets, for it expresses itself depending on our individual resources and temperament. For example, we can give help to people lovingly and compassionately just by giving them our time.

To realize this blessing, therefore, we should ask ourselves where we can most effectively employ our abilities and possessions for the benefit of others – we have, after all, only borrowed them. We should also, perhaps, ask ourselves what limits our generosity. Do we really want to support others, or do we prefer to let the professionals deal with that side of things? Have we perhaps persuaded ourselves that the world is full of evil anyway, and that it cannot be put right? This is no doubt true, but it does not relieve us of our duty to help. And then, how far do I extend my offer to help? Only up to a certain point, or am I prepared to give unconditionally?

The Buddha discussed generosity (the Pāli word is *dāna*) on many occasions. The daily practice of generosity brings inner happiness. It helps if we can give appropriately as well as generously, so ideally generosity is combined with wisdom. But even if we are not sure how worthy a character the recipient may be, giving is always better than holding on to what we have. As the saying goes, 'the more you give, the more you hold.'

To see the truth of this, we need to practise it. It does not take long to notice that there is actually an infinite store of good things, to which in principle everyone has access. The more we feel connected with all beings, and the more we pass on instead of holding on, the greater the number of people who will benefit, because the doors are open.

This is not going to happen without some courage – but then courage is necessary to the spiritual life anyway. We have to take an honest view of ourselves and our assumptions – everything with which we are familiar – examine how we spend our time, and ask ourselves, is this all there is to life?

Generosity is the first of the ten virtues listed by the Buddha. This does not make the others any less important, but it is generosity that opens the doors to them. Through generosity we learn to let go of ourselves. It is neither enjoyable nor fruitful to be concerned with oneself all the time. It's like a snake biting its tail – an eternal vicious circle. If we want to experience connectedness and solidarity with the world, it will be much easier if we practise generosity. According to the Buddha's analysis, ego-centredness is the root of our problems and our suffering. All his teachings aim to help us recognize the ego as an illusion and to let go of it. Generosity tops the list because it is the first step in overcoming the ego. It is not that we actually lose the ego by being generous; indeed, it retains its importance. But for that moment we do not have to attend to its needs. A completely different level of satisfaction can be found simply by bringing joy to others, by sharing with others. The fact that we experience joy through generosity, when our satisfaction usually comes from receiving what we desire, suggests that what we experience must indeed be a completely different level of satisfaction.

Next comes the blessing of right living, or the good life, the upright or honourable life. The Buddha never suggested that everyone should spend their life in solitary meditation. So how should we describe the right way to live? It means first of all providing for one's family and, secondly, supporting others. The Buddha suggested that people leading a worldly life should divide their income into four. One portion is for oneself and one's family, the second to keep one's business going, the third saved for hard times, and the fourth can be distributed to those leading a religious life, the sick, and the needy. This division of income is one that takes account of all our responsibilities. The sums involved are not the issue, so much as the intention.

Right living or right livelihood includes a commitment to ethical conduct. It means not causing any harm to others, whether in our actions, speech, or emotions and thoughts. The harm we do may be physical or verbal in immediate terms, but it originates in our thoughts and emotions. So ethical conduct means not bearing any ill will towards other beings. Our thoughts are not duty-free – they always carry a hidden levy, in that they form the basis of our speech and actions, and indeed constitute the ultimate or primary conditioning factor for our whole existence. We are what we think. It is not only what we do that matters, but also what kind of thoughts we cultivate. Can we say that our thoughts measure up to the highest standards?

Once more, the Buddha raises the blessing of caring; and here it is for relatives, friends, acquaintances, and colleagues. In the course of cultivating this attitude, readiness to give actual support of whatever kind should become second nature, so that we will eventually be able to treat everyone we encounter with practical care. Initially, though, we should not expect too much from ourselves, and keep cultivating this attitude.

Whenever we have any kind of dealings with another person, we should ask ourselves whether we're really interested in them, or only in ourselves. Do we appreciate the extent to which we depend on one another? Are we aware how powerfully we are affected and supported by the moods, ideas, words, and actions of others?

Nobody can truly say that they manage their life on their own. Our daily life depends on all kinds of services, like water and electricity, commerce and agriculture. We are also connected to others through our thoughts and emotions – whether we openly declare them or not. They are no less real for being unspoken, and can still have an effect on the thoughts and emotions of others. This is the blessing of caring for others. Whether others actually experience this care is another matter: the crucial thing to start with is the nurturing of those good intentions.

Making good karma means being on our guard against negativity entering our thoughts, speech, or actions. Thoughts require particular attention because that is where things start. All our actions produce results that affect ourselves as well as others, and most people produce a mixture of positive and negative results. It is rare for someone to make only bad karma, but of course too many unskilful actions will result in a prison sentence. It is equally impossible for someone to make only good karma – unless they are

Enlightened, in which case they are no longer making any bad karma because they no longer live under the illusion of an ego-based consciousness.

Our negative mental states have a grave impact on our emotional life, and we can do something to prevent them from arising just by paying attention to our changing mental states. As simple as this may sound, very few people actually make a practice of paying attention to their inner life. Only if we bring a fully committed practice of mindfulness to our self-awareness will we experience consistently positive inner states. Watching our thoughts, words, and actions even as we think, speak, and perform them will not get in the way of fulfilling the other duties of our daily life. On the contrary, the more we watch ourselves, the more one-pointed will be our concentration on whatever we are doing.

The karmic results we experience have a strong influence on the quality of our moods and emotions, and if we observe these moods it will quickly become clear where they come from: why it is that we are happy or sad. We can then change the unwholesome things we think, speak, and do that give rise to negative experience, but we can do this only if we see ourselves as we really are.

In his discourses the Buddha returns again and again to the creation of good karma. He does this because, so long as we assume, like all unenlightened beings, that we have a personal identity, we create karma with every thought that passes through our minds. But once we have understood this, we do become more mindful of our thoughts – and this is the important thing, even if we do not manage to catch all the thoughts flashing through our mind.

Refraining from unskilful things, avoiding intoxicants, being untiring in all good things. These truly are great blessings!

Again, this is all about karma and ethical precepts. The better we succeed in avoiding what our conscience reminds us is unskilful, and in doing what we know to be skilful, the more intensely will we experience this blessing. In fact, it is we ourselves who bestow it. And this is a wonderful thing – to realize that we can achieve happiness through our own efforts, without the need to wait for someone else to give us happiness, without feeling we have to get something that will make us happy. Everything can be found within.

We have a natural guide to our actions in our own conscience and emotional states. Difficulties arise, however, from our belief that we have special rights, the attitude that says, in effect, 'This is my due and if I don't get it, I'll take it.' In order to avoid the unskilful, the first thing we have to learn is to distinguish clearly between what is skilful and what is unskilful, and the more closely we observe ourselves, the easier this will become.

We are lucky to have been born as human beings, under extremely favourable conditions in which materially we lack nothing. With the benefit of such good fortune it becomes our duty to centre our life on spiritual growth rather than the insatiable demands of the ego-centred mind for so much that is unnecessary. The Buddha lists just four basic necessities: food, clothing, a roof over one's head, and medicine. Beyond these, our only aim as a human being should be to grasp the opportunity, through spiritual practice, to develop clarity of mind and breadth of awareness, with a view to one day experiencing ourselves not as separate, private individuals but as part of a whole, of all that comes and goes in the world in which we find ourselves. With this understanding of our true situation, it will also become clear how important it is to commit ourselves whole-heartedly to spiritual growth in this lifetime.

This particular discourse introduces the most basic and obvious principles for our practice. These do not involve anything unusual or require special abilities, nor do they describe anything esoteric or require special skills. They simply show us how we can live our day-to-day life. What is there other than the life we must live today? This day we must live through is everything we have. Everything else is fantasy. So every day we are to keep stepping back from the unskilful, as well as resist intoxicants: they can bring about a feeling of well-being, but meditation and spiritual practice are simpler and less problematic ways to achieve this. From the number of scriptural references to intoxicants, we can assume that people had the same problems 2,500 years ago as we have today. Nothing much has changed here.

'Being untiring in all good things' refers to training not simply in ethical behaviour but also in the Buddha's teaching generally, and for this, of course, we need information. It is not necessary to be familiar with all the teachings – in the Theravāda tradition alone there are 17,500 discourses. The basic principles and terms we have touched on, like karma and the moral precepts, are sufficient in themselves to enable us to base whatever we do on the Dhamma. In this endeavour we are not subscribing to religious ideas, but simply bringing our lives into harmony with profoundly universal truths, or laws, that we can apply for ourselves.

We have entered upon the Dhamma only if we do not centre on our own problems all the time. When we analyse our problems, we will soon find they cannot be solved on a personal level. If, instead of trying to understand them individually, we try to see their relevance for all human beings, we draw closer to the truth. The Dhamma is a universal truth, and being untiring in good things it will always lead us back to this basic fact. If we recognize that our problems are part of our human nature, we will view ourselves much more objectively and find solutions much more easily. As long as we continue to view our problems as particular to ourselves, they will continue to trouble us in one guise or another.

Reverence and humility, contentment and gratitude, to hear the Dhamma at the right time. These truly are great blessings!

The emotional qualities associated with reverence and humility play an important role in the spiritual life. Humility is a subject to which Christianity – indeed, any of the world religions – often returns, and anything that features in all the world religions is without doubt not only important but also difficult to practise. (One only need think of the five precepts or the ten commandments.)

Humility is something that arises naturally. It is completely different from an inferiority complex: humility is often confused with obsequiousness, with judging oneself or accepting a judgement of oneself as smaller, uglier, or less accomplished than others. Such a judgement is based on hierarchy and status, and whether we measure people according to class or according to economic or academic criteria. This can have nothing to do with being truly human. Humility is about the courage to bow down. The opposite is arrogance, the course of exalting oneself. To bow down before the teaching, and before other people, helps to make us receptive and pliant right to the core; it engenders an attitude that softens the ego. The stronger our ego-centredness, the harder we will find it to bow down. Humility implies not self-disdain, but self-respect. True humanity is respect for our common humanity, a respect for oneself and others, and it manifests through sincere and humble conduct.

As well as being a reflection of true humanity, humility includes the knowledge that there is something higher to which we can aspire. When we transcend the human level and see ourselves in all our true insignificance, confined as our experience is to the narrow boundaries of individual consciousness, we become aware of the true nature of the universe. If we humbly acknowledge that there is something higher than us, we will be able to give ourselves to it; and without completely giving and committing ourselves in this way, we will not be able to meditate. Humility and commitment therefore go together. Someone who is too convinced of his importance and wants to hold on to that conviction, cannot give himself. But once we have understood in all humility that there is something that goes beyond our ordinary experience and vision, we can give ourselves totally to meditative and contemplative experience. Humility is therefore an essential quality and a great blessing.

Accompanying humility in this discourse is reverence. As we have seen, reverence or respect is not something we are familiar with nowadays. For whom do we feel reverence? To whom do we pay honour? All too often it is pop stars or sports idols, but these are certainly not the objects of reverence meant here. We have to realize that only something that reaches far beyond our human existence and our everyday experience can truly inspire reverence and respect in our hearts. We need the spiritual understanding to pay honour to that which is highest, and we express this reverence by bowing before a statue of the Buddha. Not that one is bowing to the statue itself: one bows to it inasmuch as the image of the Buddha represents the quintessence of Enlightenment in every human being. This action helps to instil in us reverence and respect. Our life can never be as perfect as we wish, it never satisfies us completely, but with knowledge of something higher we can live with that.

Following these come two more positive emotional qualities that are great blessings: contentment and gratitude. Most people feel grateful when they receive something new, but forget to be grateful for what they already have. It is as well to remind ourselves more often of all the good things we experience, and not just take them for granted. When we are ill we long for nothing more ardently than to be well, but when we are healthy we look upon good health as something unremarkable. When we are hungry we will be grateful for any food we can get, but as long as we are getting enough to eat we are likely to be very picky about our food. Gratitude can be cultivated in any situation. For example, instead of complaining about people's faults, we can be grateful for their qualities. Gratitude is an emotional response that is humble and full of devotion and love.

The Buddha makes frequent mention of the quality of contentment, as it is naturally conducive to peace. Most people want to find peace, without knowing where or how to look for it. Most obviously, they blame political systems or individual politicians for their lack of peace. But peace is a quality of the heart, available to anyone through their own efforts, and found only by one who is content.

If we are content with the people around us and the situations we find ourselves in, we will have fewer desires. Each individual desire we express brings us dissatisfaction, known in Pāli as *dukkha*. The more we wish our circumstances to be different, the more dissatisfied we become. If we examine our life, it will become readily apparent that we can never be satisfied by all that it holds. All the changes we would like to see lie outside our direct control, leaving us dependent on other people or external circumstances for their realization, with the result that a real solution is simply not feasible. The only way truly to change something is to change ourselves. Once we have effected a change in ourselves, everything will be completely different.

Contentment will lead to Enlightenment, and it can be experienced in meditative absorption. Through such experience we come clearly to recognize that contentment is only possible in the absence of craving. Only when we feel no further need to change ourselves and others, when we realize that nothing that exists can ever be made perfect on that basis and the process of change has to take place within ourselves, will peace be possible. We should not need to experience discontent even with our failure to attain these states; on the contrary, we should simply be glad to have found a way to enter the spiritual life.

So these attributes of the spiritual life – gratitude and contentment – impart a quality of peace to our life. Much of the *Mahāmaṅgala Sutta* is concerned with positive feelings and emotions such as these, which may arise in the context of how we live, act, and deal with

other people, and they can be, according to the Buddha, great
blessings in our lives. And there are more to follow.

Next comes 'hearing the truth at the right time,' which is about
being ready and receptive. The Dhamma itself is a blessing only if
we hear it at the right time. Most people who hear about the
Dhamma are not ready for it, but this does not mean they will never
be ready for it. On the other hand, they might *not* hear the Dhamma
when they are ready for it. Therefore, as we cannot guarantee
hearing the Dhamma again in future, we must do our best to make
this present moment the right time, by being as receptive as possible
and making the most of what we can learn now.

> *Having patience, being receptive and unreactive when*
> *corrected, seeking the presence of the wise, discussing the*
> *truth. These truly are great blessings!*

First, then, comes patience – and this is a great blessing indeed. Most
people vacillate between patience and impatience. Taken to an ex-
treme, impatience indicates that we insist on having things our own
way. As things rarely go all our own way, impatience throws us into
a state of painful unrest.

Patience implies an understanding that all things are impermanent, an awareness that everything we perceive is in flux, be it our
own feelings or emotions, our experience of the moment, or our
sense of today or of our whole life. We cannot hold on to anything
because everything disappears. Since we try again and again to hold
on to things, we experience constant disappointment. It is easy to
lose sight of this truth that nothing lasts, because some things happen repeatedly, as though the same thing keeps coming back, but
these events are only similar. Take our breath, for instance. Each
breath disappears as soon as it is drawn and released, but because
each new breath is similar to the previous one we prefer not to notice
that our breath is impermanent, and that therefore we ourselves are
impermanent. Without our breath, we could not live, and its impermanence shows the fragility of our existence: if the breath stops,
death rapidly follows. According to the Buddha, most of us prefer
not to think about this because of our ego delusion.

We always seem to be trying to make permanent all this evidence
of universal impermanence, and to regard these impermanent

things that must bring suffering when they pass away as pleasant. Yet the transitory nature of each thought, each feeling, each bodily movement, can be observed every second. Everything will be lost; nothing remains as it is. There are many ways of keeping things available – writing, photography, film, and memory – but if we imagine we can actually hold on to people, emotions, experiences, or events, we will be left holding on to emptiness. If, on the other hand, we come to understand that nothing lasts, the patience we experience as a result will come with a sense of relief and tranquillity. We shall stop feeling the need to interfere.

We all know we need perseverance to maintain our meditation, but we need patience, too: without it our meditation will never bear fruit. Very few of us are able to meditate straight away. But not only should we push ourselves, we need to be patient with ourselves, again and again, day after day.

If one can be more patient with oneself, it will be easier to be patient with others, especially when things are not going to plan. The alternative produces a rigid and intractable attitude towards both ourselves and others. It is clear, therefore, that patience goes hand in hand with loving-kindness, and that the cultivation of patience is a great blessing.

Our greatest potential lies in our capacity to learn. We can get anything we want if we focus sufficient thought and effort on it. This is not to say that we can have everything our own way. If we think that, we will be banging our head against a brick wall. But if we wish to be patient we will eventually develop patience. The possibility of following the path recommended by the Buddha, and of attaining its goal, is there for anyone – anyone who wants it and works for it. 'Where there's a will, there's a way,' as the saying goes. Because we usually do get what we really want, we just have to take care that what we want is skilful.

The next blessing is 'being receptive and unreactive when corrected'. Being receptive to criticism does not come easily to people. Not getting angry or upset, or criticizing in return, obviously has a lot to do with patience, but it is also a matter of confidence, and many people hold themselves in such low esteem that if a critical remark confirms their negative self-view, they become angry, or at least unhappy.

Our weaknesses are mostly hidden – otherwise we'd have corrected our faults already. So to be corrected by the voice of wisdom is a great blessing. Understanding ourselves and learning to behave more skilfully is much easier with help from others, but we do have to be prepared to accept that help. Conversely, if we want to help someone, we can usually sense whether they are open to constructive criticism, but we should not try to give help if it is clear they are not receptive. It is important to be able to accept both possibilities, offering criticism when it is of use, and being happy to refrain when it isn't. Perfection exists only beyond the human realm. Within the human realm, needless to say, there is room for improvement in everyone, and therefore every justification for helpful criticism.

Of course, criticism can sometimes be unjustified. If it is, we are not obliged to heed it, and we definitely shouldn't be upset by it. We can even be grateful that someone has taken the trouble to tell us what they think – for gratitude can be, as we have seen, a blessing in itself.

Following on from this is 'seeking the company of the wise and discussing the truth'. This is another blessing that the Buddha frequently stresses elsewhere: that of noble friends and noble conversation. The topics of our talk constitute the nourishment for our mind. The more nutritious the food, the more beneficial it is to the mind. Speaking about the truth is not just about making sure that everything we say is literally true. It requires us to discuss matters beyond our day-to-day concerns in order to go deeper in getting to know people, including ourselves. It should be concerned with the universal truth that is accessible to all of us. Such truth is not to be confused with scientific truth – such as how the universe functions – which has never helped anyone to become really loving and helpful in the way the universal spiritual truth of the Dhamma does. So discussion of the Dhamma is clearly a great blessing. Of course, this is not to say we should never talk about everyday matters; only that we should recognize them for the mundane necessities they are, and not mistake them for that which constitutes our real life.

All that really counts takes place within ourselves, in our reactions, wishes, plans, and hopes. What do we really look forward to, what do we intend, what do we really want? Are we searching for the highest truth, for the ultimate goal, for that which transforms us and takes us beyond our human condition? Or are we stuck in our everyday life, just hoping to muddle through a bit better?

Once we seek the company of the wise and discuss the truth we have begun a spiritual quest in search of truths other than the mundane, and in search of human beings who can provide us with the best help on our spiritual quest. Only spiritual truth shows us the way by which all grief and sorrow may eventually be eradicated. However, although such truths are accessible to anyone, few of us are prepared to follow them. This is because they do not look the way we would like them to look: they are concerned with impermanence and utter dissolution. They tell us that the only fruit of grasping and rejection is sorrow, and they recommend that we rein in the ego until we can unmask it as an illusion. Everyone would like to experience happiness, peace, and harmony within, and everyone wants to retain their ego. But there can be an end to sorrow only when we give up the ego, and it is because most people fall short of this objective that there is so little peace and happiness in the world.

'Approaching the wise and discussing the truth' shows us where to find peace: true peace comes only from within; it begins in the heart and radiates out from there. However, although there is only one place to find peace, everyone has all they need to find it and develop it. In the outside world there is ultimately no peace: there is always something not quite right which has to be changed or attended to. On the spiritual plane, by contrast, there is an inner acceptance of things as they are. If we submit ourselves to these truths, and flow with them, we will reap the fruits of this great blessing.

> *Self-surrender and purification, insight into the noble truths,*
> *finally Enlightenment itself, these truly are great blessings!*

As we practise, we learn to surrender ourselves by purifying the heart, that is, by cultivating positive emotions, purifying the intellect, and clarifying and deepening our thinking. Without this blessing of inner purification there can be no self-surrender. We know from experience how we suffer and how miserable we get when we think or feel negatively. It hurts us, and often hurts others too. Unfortunately, we are not always prepared to admit that the necessary change must come from us. Most of us are convinced that external conditions are responsible and that changes have to be made to our situation to spare us from our negativity.

Nearly everyone thinks along these lines. We want to change anything but ourselves. And what is the outcome? Not a lot! Some situations might be improved, but it is primarily our own thoughts and feelings that we have to change in order to find peace. To this end we need constantly to practise mindfulness, establishing it in meditation and sustaining it in daily life. We need to keep careful watch over ourselves in order not to miss any opportunity for purification – after all, no one else is going to do it for us.

Purification is not about lifestyle – our accoutrements or lack of them – but about the quality of life, the way it is lived. And purification is of course a gradual process; it is happening the moment we try it – whatever the actual results. Everyone comes up against difficulties – things never work out the way we plan – but this is no reason to be depressed and resentful. On the contrary, it is an occasion for joy, inasmuch as we have become aware of what is going on inside.

If we keep replacing unskilful thoughts and emotions with skilful ones, we will soon recognize that self-surrender is the only possible solution to the human condition. But this is something we have to find out for ourselves. The wisdom of others can be of some help, but it is only a pointer, not a personal experience, and it is only by means of purification that we will make it our own.

The further the process goes, the clearer is the picture we have of ourselves, and the clearer it becomes that everything going on in us has to do with the ego, that unyielding sense of wanting something. The ego considers itself important and wants to be the centre of attention. As we look at ourselves and work on ourselves, it becomes ever clearer that the only way to purify ourselves is by subjecting that person who appears to be residing in our being to a more and more subtle analysis.

Are we able to see that this ego is just a thought? All of us believe that 'me' is somebody important, who needs protection, and wants to keep some things and get rid of others. This somebody insists on taking centre stage, and runs into difficulties with others who claim the spotlight. We need look no further than this for the origin of all the problems in our relationships. They are brought about less by unacceptable conduct than by the clash of two egos.

The blessing that arises once we have seen through this illusion is a discovery so overwhelming that the Buddha called it Enlightenment, and if we can get some inkling of it ourselves, we will have made a good start. Becoming aware of the illusion within ourselves means detecting a flaw in the way we make sense of things. This flaw is deeply rooted in the mind, but if we are able to eliminate it and cease to experience ourselves as this absolutely separate identity, all suffering will cease.

The elimination of ego-illusion is not easy; it will be possible only by realizing that there is no other way to overcome dukkha. The ego has its own ideas: 'I want my happiness,' it says, and it thinks it knows where to look for it. As long as we follow the ego in our search for happiness, whether through using meditation merely to calm ourselves instead of using it as a tool for insight, a pleasant social life, solitary retreats, or other activities, we will not be able to get to grips with this illusion. Only if the mind says 'no me, no my, nothing but dedication, humility, and impermanence', will we be on the right track. When we are able to surrender the self, to let go, at least momentarily, we will experience for that moment untold joy and ease, as if all our burdens had fallen away, giving us a glimpse of what it means to renounce the ego. This does not happen overnight; it arises on the path of purification, upon which we constantly try to recognize dukkha as the result of our ego-illusion.

The blessing that follows is insight into the four noble truths, which together constitute the Buddha's explanation of the Enlightenment he experienced under the celebrated bodhi tree in Bodhgaya, some 2,500 years ago. They provide an answer to the basic existential questions. What is the reason for suffering? Why are we unfulfilled and discontented? It is not because – as we tend to think – we cannot get what we want or because we are not loved and respected. The one and only reason is that existence means dukkha. This is the gist of the first noble truth: life is never quite as we would like it to be. The second noble truth elucidates the origin of this suffering and discontent, which is that we crave change. We do not want to accept life the way it is; we do not want to let go and be part of the flow; we want to dig in our heels and assert ourselves. This is why we are dissatisfied and unfulfilled, and this is the second noble truth: the truth of the cause of suffering.

The third noble truth is that of Enlightenment, that suffering can be overcome. The fourth is the way to that goal, the noble eightfold path, comprising the three great elements into which the Buddha divides his teaching: *sīla, samādhi,* and *paññā*: ethical conduct, meditative concentration, and wisdom or insight. These three elements are the pillars upon which purification and self-surrender are supported. Whether we practise them, and to what degree, is entirely up to us; nevertheless, we cannot but be extremely grateful for a teaching that explains the way so clearly and gives us instructions for our practice.

'Enlightenment itself, that is a great blessing.' From beginning to end, this discourse deals with the path to Enlightenment: the importance of conversing with noble people – not with fools, but with the wise. And living in quiet surroundings, bearing in mind our higher aspirations and not limiting ourselves to the concerns of daily life.

People often raise the objection: 'but I don't have time for all that!' But what is time? Time is not what we see when we look at a clock. Time only appears to be limited. The time we actually have cannot be calculated; it is a question of making proper use of it. In every action, every thought, every passing feeling, we can realize our aspirations. We do not need any extra time for that. The time we have is now, in every moment. If we have taken on board a spiritual aspiration, we can express it in the ordinary actions, thoughts, and feelings of this very day. Not having enough time is beside the point. Such reasoning is based on the delusion that happiness can be found within the world. The best the world can offer is pleasure – which needs to be renewed over and over again, whereas true happiness is found in the heart and is eternal. We all have it; we need only to discover it.

> *A heart not trembling – sorrowless, stainless, and secure –*
> *even when touched by the eight worldly phenomena. This is*
> *a great blessing.*

The eight worldly phenomena that tend to make the heart tremble are the eight worldly experiences of gain and loss, respect and contempt, praise and blame, pleasure and pain. We all come across these from time to time, but it is because we are conditioned to welcome the four agreeable poles of experience, and to reject the four disagreeable ones, that we can never find peace. We constantly look for what seems favourable and flinch from adversity, and because everyone does the same, there is no peace in the world. Peace will arrive only when we have ceased to be lured by the four comforts and ceased to recoil from the four discomforts. Only when we have accepted that these opposites give rise to each other can we live a balanced life.

We have to recognize that the positive in our experience is as impermanent as anything else. Whatever we get hold of, be it money, love, another human being, a joyful event, it is impermanent. Just as it came to be, so will it cease. To accept this requires not only a deep understanding of impermanence, but complete equanimity. If, for example, we bury our experience of loss, yet take pleasure in gaining something else, it is clear we do not have this understanding. We need to keep looking impermanence in the eye, acknowledging it and realizing how short is our time on this earth and how insignificant we are compared to all creation. What makes the difference is our commitment to purification and our moment-to-moment conduct, a heart full of love and a readiness to support others. This helps us to face the eight worldly conditions from a detached perspective so that they no longer have any power over us.

'A heart not trembling, even when touched by the eight worldly phenomena' means accepting each phenomenon with the same equanimity, with no preferences or aversions. This is a major step, and a difficult one: we should not expect to be able to do it all in one go, but at least let us practise. Just by appreciating the superfluity of all our yearnings and aversions – how they are there one minute and gone the next, how they ebb and flow – we are practising equanimity.

Equanimity is one of the seven factors leading to Enlightenment, and is not to be confused with indifference. Equanimity is a deep insight with an unshakeable heart full of love. Indifference is the cold shoulder, the way we avoid getting involved – and end up making life even more difficult. Equanimity is the highest of all emotions and requires courage. The Latin root of the word means 'even' (*aequus*) 'mind' or 'courage' (*animus*). It requires the courage to be different, to refuse to take sides, to resist losing one's vision in the dazzle of the world.

The world does have this extraordinary tendency to lead us astray, and the Buddha's terminology reflects this fact with the word *māra*, or 'tempter' (often translated in the West as 'devil'). Māra is always present in us, for, as Faust puts it, 'two souls, alas! are dwelling in my breast'. The world appears to our eyes as though it can satisfy us. But though we may admire a beautiful rainbow, in what sense can it give us what we really want? It cannot: it has the most fascinating colours, but nobody can ever possess it.

It is the same with the world. It fascinates us with its colourful splendour, but it is not something anyone can actually possess. All we can truly possess lies within us, which has been there for ever. Our main task, therefore, is inner purification, recognizing the delusion of ego and all our useless reactions to the eight worldly phenomena: gain and loss, respect and contempt, praise and blame, pleasure and pain.

The heart 'sorrowless, stainless, and secure' is the Enlightened mind. These characteristics describe Enlightened beings. It hardly needs to be said that they are purified and know no sorrows, but they also feel completely secure, because no egotism remains to feel threatened. Such perfect security results from recognizing, and letting go of, the illusion.

> *Those who attain that are invincible at all times and all places. They find happiness everywhere, and this is the supreme blessing.*

The whole discourse on the thirty-eight blessings aims to show us where to find true happiness – not temporary happiness, which can be lost, but a form of happiness that remains with us and is completely secure. Enlightened beings cannot lose their inner happiness because there is no longer anyone there to gain or lose anything. There is only heart, mind, and body, which will continue to function as long as there is sufficient vital energy. Such beings are invincible always and everywhere and experience the supreme blessing.

Whether we gradually approach this happiness depends entirely on us. If we consider that the world takes priority, and imagine we have important business to carry out there, we will certainly not have enough time for our spiritual progress, which will take second place.

Withdrawal from the business of the world is not withdrawal of love from our hearts. It means only that we become free from attachment. If we have really chosen this path, it will be worth analysing our attachments, and making a list of them, assessing what we are most attached to, whether people, things, experiences, youth, or beauty. Are there some we are able to loosen, or is the attachment too powerful and established for us to let go? Alternatively, we might ask ourselves: 'What are my strongest aversions? What do I most hate? What do I most want to change?' These things are, of course, simply mirror images of our attachments, with everything reversed.

Before the Buddha became Enlightened, he fathered a son he called Rāhula, which means 'fetter' – that is to say, the fetter of attachment. As long as we are attached to the world, as long as we want to have things and keep them, we are bound in fetters. We want everything to stay in order, and not to change. Each of us lives in the grip of our attachments, and the strongest of them all is attachment to ourselves. We may like to believe that other people are more important to us than ourselves, but if we were no longer attached to ourselves we would be able to let go of others more easily. That our attachments produce negative emotions and difficulties for us should be obvious to anyone, and any training that helps us become more aware of them must clearly be valuable.

However we go about our practice, we must try to redirect our thoughts from the repetitive (and usually rather boring) activities of our daily lives, towards those things that embody and express real values. Fundamental to this process of self-surrender and self-purification is the practice of meditation. Though not sufficient on its own, it is still absolutely necessary.

The many blessings enumerated in this text assist us in the aim of one day shaking off the last trammels of dukkha and becoming so free that our mind is no longer oppressed by anything. They all contribute to inner happiness and peace and accompany us on our path towards final liberation.

Keep the company of noble friends
Who live a pure life, who are not lethargic.
Be friendly wherever you are.
Always be prudent in all your actions.
Then, filled with bliss you will
Make an end to all suffering.

Dhammapada 376

3

An End to All Suffering

IN THE GROUP of six lines from the *Dhammapada* quoted opposite can be found the key to the cessation of all suffering.

Keep the company of noble friends
Who live a pure life, who are not lethargic.

The first instruction, concerning spiritual friendship, is a recurring theme in the Buddha's teaching, because we are so easily influenced by the company we keep. A 'noble friend' is a friend who is not lethargic, and who in his daily life does not indulge in even small excesses. In other words, someone who leads a pure and energetic life. Unless we are able to observe in a friend such an exemplary tenor of life over an extended period, we cannot speak of them as a noble or spiritual friend in the truest sense. The Buddha said that we can know a person thoroughly only once we have lived with them for a long period; one commentary specifies twelve years.

The decisive factor in allowing us a view of someone's spiritual practice or inner conduct is not what they say, but the way they live their life. Talk is one thing, action quite another – and the two can often diverge very considerably in one person. Conversation with a noble friend brings us fresh insights regarding our spiritual path inasmuch as such a friend is engaged in leading a spiritual life themselves, and will have a fresh clarity to offer because their priority will always be spiritual development rather than the worldly life.

This clarity will naturally express itself in simple terms that will awaken in us new perspectives and deeper understanding. The Buddha is recorded as having said that his teaching should be expounded in as simple a form as possible, in order to make it accessible to as many people as possible. No one should go away with the idea that they are not capable of understanding it; nor should anyone imagine that all they need do is believe in the teaching. Neither of these attitudes is helpful.

According to the Buddha, we can confide in a good friend without fear or hesitation in the knowledge that they will not disclose our secrets. We can of course do this only if we know we will do the same for them: trust has to be mutual. A good friend will always make sure that others do not speak ill of us, and will always be pleased to hear good things about us.

Communication provides a fundamental sustenance for the mind. That is why it is important to be with people whose speech has a spiritual dimension to it. We might need to talk about everyday business, of course, and a noble friend might be able to provide good worldly advice, but that shouldn't take all day. The mind has its own needs, which are to be nourished, refined, inspired, and towards which the company of a good friend can make a more significant contribution, helping us to feel joyful and confirmed in our faith.

The Buddha went so far as to say that a good friend makes all the difference in the spiritual life. The significance of a noble friend is stressed right at the start of this verse, as the first condition for putting an end to suffering. If we know someone who can help us on this path, who encourages what is skilful in us and whom we can emulate, then we are truly fortunate, and we should do all we can to become closer to them and cultivate their company.

People have a much stronger influence on us than we generally realize. When we are talking to people who do not have a spiritual practice, it is easy to slip on to their level, unless we have trained our mind to try to draw them on to ours. This requires the initial development of a high degree of mindfulness, hence the emphasis the Buddha places on being with people who have this ability to help us on the path. We need our own intellectual faculty, indicated here by the word 'prudent'. Our actions must always be governed by foresight and good judgement, by an inner voice that speaks loud and clear from our conscience and reminds us, for example, that we have to be able to distinguish between friends who are noble and those who are not. But in our laziness or short-sightedness that inner voice can get ignored, because we have another inner voice – that of our desire – which gains our attention more easily, and to which we are inclined to give in rather too readily.

We may try to justify our actions by pointing out that everyone does the same thing. It has to be understood, however, that the spiritual path is totally different from the ways of materialism, and that the conduct of the majority offers no kind of guide to what is actually right conduct. Rather, if we take a careful and honest look at most people, we can probably conclude that the purely worldly path does not really work for them, even on its own terms.

We will dig up any number of excuses when we want to suffocate the inner voice that points us in the direction of the skilful and virtuous. Even while it is making itself clearly heard, we still say, 'Well, why not? What harm would it really do? I have the right to do it. Other people do it. It would so much more convenient to do it.'

Such sophistry and evasion has to be exposed over and over again. We have to keep reminding ourselves, one way or another, where our true interests lie. We can, for example, visualize friends and enemies – and also the noble friend – as existing somehow within ourselves. We can then choose to be our own best friend rather than our worst enemy. We can do this just by listening carefully to ourselves for the advice that will make us truly happy; not in an egocentric sense of living from one pleasure to the next – which of course has nothing to do with happiness – but in the sense of joy coming from within, which is what everyone is truly seeking.

Though the Buddha is concerned here with our attitude towards noble friends, it is also important to consider our attitude towards ourselves: to consider, through self-observation, whether we are truly our own best friend. Are we aware of the conversation taking place in our mind? If so, can we recognize the direction and drift of our thoughts, and do we know how to work with them?

Whatever happens around us, it is our thoughts that determine the quality of our inner lives. We ourselves have brought about all that happens there. Only when we have accepted this as a fact and are willing to live with its implications, can we really say we are following a spiritual path. I alone am responsible for my happiness and peace – and for my unhappiness and disquiet as well. Until we have understood this, we will always be looking for happiness outside ourselves. Conversely, if we experience something unpleasant we look for a scapegoat, and there are plenty to choose from. It is easy enough to find something or someone to blame, whether on our doorstep or far away. So long as we do this, so long as we expect happiness from external circumstances or regard these as the cause of unhappiness, we are still stuck on a material level of being, acting in basically the same way as everyone else.

The real shift comes when we realize that our thoughts are what make us happy or unhappy, that they are the masters of our inner life. Then we will make sure we are our own best friend – even our own noble friend – whatever our external circumstances might be. As a noble friend to ourselves, we will support all that is positive in us, while dissuading ourselves from the negative, and we will foster an interest in anything that can help us make progress. Again and again we will patiently acknowledge our difficulties, and instead of blaming ourselves we will try to change something.

If we deal with our own weaknesses compassionately, we will feel the same compassion towards others, and recognize their difficulties. Through being compassionate we cultivate an inner nobility of spirit. In this way, we can leave behind everyday concerns, the market-place mentality, and feelings of aversion and negativity, and try to lift our spirit, our mental states, and our emotions to a level where we can recognize everything as universal process.

It helps if we can avoid viewing events purely from our own point of view. If we can resist the tendency always to consider how 'I' would prefer it, how 'I' would like to change it, we can experience ourselves as part of the bigger picture instead. Nor is it enough just to talk about this way of looking at things; we need to do some serious thinking – thinking that goes to the root of our feelings and shapes our inner life. In this way, too, we build up our independence and self-reliance. Important as it is to elicit help, we should also be trying to monitor and direct our progress ourselves.

Something particularly interesting about the Buddha's teaching is that it consists only of instructions and guidelines. Everyone has to make their own way, and try things out for themselves. The more we practise, and the less reluctant we are, harbouring fewer aversions, the more deeply we will realize that this is a pragmatic teaching entirely consistent with reason, and that it does truly enable us eventually to let go of all suffering.

A change in our way of thinking is indispensable if we are to achieve that end, and there is a very simple way to describe that change: instead of wanting things we must give them up. On the level of the market place, when we want something we are willing to pay for it, but not a penny more than we think it's worth. On the spiritual level it's totally different: there is nothing to get, and whatever we drag around with us – opinions and views, hopes and wishes, reluctance and aversion – has to be abandoned. This letting go starts with skilful thinking or reflection, what the Buddha called 'wise consideration', and through it a purity can arise within us by which we can clearly identify what is highest in our nature. We have to be able to do this because we can only live out those values with which we are in contact in ourselves. We have to find the teaching within ourselves.

The word 'noble' has a special meaning in Buddhism, and refers to someone who has succeeded in internalizing the teaching in this way. There are a number of stages on the way to this goal. We might at first hear a teaching and forget it. Then we may hear it and make a point of remembering it. If we remember it we can go on to practise it. And finally we can investigate whether anything has changed in the course of that practice. The path has been described clearly enough – the walking is up to us.

The self-inquiry involved in being a noble friend to ourselves requires us to know what is best for us – which is not necessarily what is most convenient or pleasant. This is especially difficult at the beginning of the spiritual path, because we are suddenly faced with things that we had no idea lay dormant within us. We need courage to see these elements of our nature without self-deception. Again, any anger, frustration, or impatience that arises during the process is incompatible with compassion and cannot do any good. Being compassionate towards ourselves and recognizing our difficulties helps us to be equally understanding towards others.

The stanza goes on to describe the ideal noble friend as living a pure life and not being lethargic. One will sometimes come across the view that a spiritual person who has to some extent internalized the teaching will spend all their time sitting on their meditation cushion, or gazing out of the window, or speaking only ten words a day. Absurd as this may sound, such opinions are not uncommon, and often firmly held. People have fierce discussions about the special way a spiritual person should lead their life, but studies of medieval Christian mystics reveal that they were particularly practical people, who mostly managed their lives very successfully.

Not being lethargic means we do what needs to be done rather than postpone it. Inertia originating in the mind naturally makes the body feel heavy as well. The mind then invents all sorts of excuses, summarized thus by the Buddha: 'The fool says, "It's too early to practise," or "It's too late," "It's too hot," or "It's too cold." He says, "I am too full," or "I'm too empty," "I'm too young," or "I'm too old."' Nowadays, we come up with other reasons: 'Just now, meditation is impossible – there's too much noise. But when the children are grown up, or once my husband retires….'

The lethargic mind is not only one that doesn't want to do anything, it is also a mind that is unable to focus on anything. It may seem very active, wandering in all directions and continuously thinking, yet very little ever comes of this activity. When the mind wanders and cannot collect itself, its discursive thinking obstructs any meditative states. It may conjure up the most beautiful stories and have wonderful day-dreams and fantasies, but they will be of little use with regard to the path as a practical proposition. Such a scattered mind will be to all intents and purposes lethargic, whereas one-pointedness is a great help in daily life, and protects the mind from feeling the need to get involved with whatever it encounters, enabling it to concentrate on what healthy human intelligence recognizes as genuinely important. Consequently, at some stage we do need to clarify what is really important in our life. What is life actually about for us? It is a good idea to think about this, and even to write it down occasionally. We may well find that this investigation leads to quite different results in the space of a few days or weeks, which makes it all the more important to keep re-examining our fundamental priorities. If lethargy tends to allow everyday business to interrupt our progress, such reminders of our goals may serve to awaken a new zest in pursuing them.

We like to tell ourselves that we are far too busy, yet we often find that people who seem to be constantly stretched to the limit actually achieve very little. Those with an agile and one-pointed mind can always do an extra bit of work if necessary. An agile mind will also prevent the body from losing its vigour, so that mind and body work together.

We have to do many things just to stay alive, and many people are occupied with these mundane tasks from morning to night. Is this effort worth so much trouble, in view of our knowledge that we are not going to live for ever? We all acknowledge that there is something more precious than daily survival, but what do we actually do from the time we open our eyes in the morning until we go to bed? Have we made any positive difference to others during the day? Have we tried at any point to prise the mind from essentially material concerns? The Buddha's teaching comprises principles and advice that can be understood and followed by anyone willing to do so. The Buddha never tried to manipulate or proselytize. Instead, he taught in simple terms and with the utmost patience, and then encouraged people to practise. Moreover, he talked to people who had the same difficulties, cravings, and dislikes that we have today. The world may have changed outwardly – technology, architecture, and fashion give us something new every day – but much has remained the same, and his teaching is as relevant as ever. Also just as relevant is the goal of deep insight into transcendental truth, unfolding a whole new perspective on the world and ourselves, which brings us eventually to the end of all pain and suffering.

Be friendly wherever you are.

On the mundane level, this may seem an impossible task, as so many people are not particularly friendly. But on the path of purification we have no choice but to be friendly. If we are unfriendly we are in that moment creating bad karma, and we will consequently feel unhappy – that is, we will feel the pangs of an uneasy conscience. There is a common and erroneous belief that karma comes only from our previous lives, and accumulated karma goes on to the next, but in fact we make karma in every conscious moment, and reap its results all the time. The present process matters much more than whatever karma we carry from the past or into the future. The past is over and the future has no existence except as a mental concept; when it arrives, it will be called the present. We make karma now, in this very moment, neither before nor after. Karma indeed has something to do with past and future, but that should not really concern us.

We can encounter the effects of karma on the spot, every day. When we feel good, peaceful, pleasant, it is very likely that we have been behaving to the best of our knowledge of what is right, that is, according to our conscience. If, on the other hand, we feel agitated, we can infer that our behaviour has not been quite as it should be: perhaps we have been unfriendly, or our thoughts have been unskilful, or we want to get hold of or get rid of something. There are plenty of excuses and explanations to draw upon that give us plausible reasons for our unskilful reactions, but they are all pointless, since none of them will ever take away that unpleasant feeling within.

In this context we should remind ourselves not to be unfriendly if someone is unfriendly towards us. In view of the fact that they are creating bad karma in that moment, we should feel compassionate rather than unfriendly. We should bear in mind that if we are unfriendly in turn we will be creating bad karma too. Most people act according to the mundane law of repaying unkindness with unkindness, and believe there is no reasonable alternative. As Buddhists, however, we are asked to undertake the course of action recommended by the Buddha: not to repay unkind and unpleasant behaviour in the same coin, but to indicate through our behaviour that there is another way. This will be of benefit to ourselves, and perhaps to the other person as well.

Always be prudent in all your actions.

This is about carefully monitoring our actions in order to avoid reacting on impulse. We are all to quick to condemn others when we see their bad side taking over, and we should be just as watchful and discriminating with our own actions. However, though it is unskilful to give way to our negative tendencies, it is also unskilful to become depressed about them.

That said, we should not be afraid to let ourselves be known to our friends as we really are, and they can only really know us if they know our behaviour in everyday life and not just on special occasions. Even while we remain mindful, our everyday behaviour should not be applied like a mask, or be based on an identification with some personality. It should come from the heart.

As well as extending to our dealings with friends, we should also bring prudence to our conduct generally in order not to make enemies unnecessarily. It seems impossible to avoid making some enemies. Even the Buddha had enemies – as did Jesus of Nazareth. So making friends will not always work out, but this is no reason not to make the attempt, not to try to make real friends, based on what we feel in our heart.

Unfortunately, we are used to speaking to people on the basis of intellectual knowledge. It would be much easier for us to get along with each other if we all spoke from the heart of our feelings, but this seems to be quite rare in everyday relationships. But it is always possible to learn something new, and the more that we develop qualities of the heart, like love and compassion, the more they will inform our communication. The more deeply our feelings go, the easier it is to express them in words, and the easier it is to make friends.

Friends are not there to boost our self-affirmation, but to give us the chance to be a noble friend. Our path of practice thus serves to support others, an important point which is emphasized again and again in the scriptures. But we can help others only in so far as we have already helped ourselves, and if our own difficulties still loom very large, we might have to work on them before we can help others.

If we surround ourselves with noble friends who lead a virtuous life and are free from sloth, and if we are friendly and prudent, we will be filled with bliss. This phrase, 'filled with bliss', might sound strange. On the most basic level it means a feeling of contentment arising from the knowledge that we have done our best, and this is an important starting-point for meditation. If we know we have done our best we will find peace of mind more easily, and know that we will generally enjoy the results of our good karma; we can be confident that our good karma is helping and supporting us. The Buddha says that we are heirs to our own karma, that if we make good karma this valuable inheritance will sustain us, and this knowledge itself contributes to our bliss.

In this way we will also find it easier to reach the first meditative absorption, which triggers the sensation of bliss. This first stage of concentration is mentioned by the Buddha in almost all his instruction on meditation. As well as bringing bliss and joy it also serves as an antidote to our negative feelings, our hatred and resentment. In feeling blissful we cannot at the same time feel resentment or hatred. Moreover, such an experience of bliss has a lasting effect.

In this verse we have an instruction about what is necessary for concentration and tranquillity outside meditation. The Buddha has been recorded elsewhere as saying that in order to meditate properly, mind and body must be at ease and the mind must be filled with joy. Only then does meditation become possible, leading towards the absorptions. When we experience these for the first time we get answers to many of our doubts. This is the beginning of the path to the ultimate extinction of all suffering.

The Buddha taught that all existence is characterized by suffering, as it can never be fulfilling or completely satisfying, but he also shows us the way to leave all suffering behind. It is sometimes claimed that the Buddha's teaching is pessimistic, because he uses the word 'suffering'. In fact, his teaching is above all realistic. He identifies our real troubles, and their close connection with impermanence. He also points out how to overcome them with the help of deep insight, insight achieved by abandoning personal opinions. We have to start by realizing that our views have never brought us any bliss, but merely bolstered our false idea that we are *someone*.

Then, filled with bliss you will
Make an end to all suffering.

Here the Buddha reassures us that we are on the way towards the end of all suffering with our very first step. The way begins in our daily life; it has an effect on our friendships, on our conduct and emotions, on the vitality and purity of our mind, and on our meditation. If we take these steps, remind ourselves again and again to avoid inertia of the mind, and be our own best friend, and if we go on to take steps to experience bliss and joy in the first absorption, then we are on the right path.

Making an end to all suffering does not mean that suffering in the world ceases but that belief in an ego ceases. There is then no one left to experience suffering. Indeed, our suffering starts to lessen on the way to this realization, as our belief in the self lessens. Making an end to the world's suffering has to begin with our own suffering, because we can only communicate what we ourselves have experienced and realized.

Easily seen are the faults of others,
Hard indeed to see are one's own;
The faults of others you bring to light
Like winnowing the chaff,
But your own faults you cover up
As the trickster conceals a losing throw.

Those who always find fault with others,
Who criticize constantly,
Their own cravings will grow,
Far are they from the cessation of their desires.

Dhammapada 252–3

4

The Faults of Others

THE TWO STANZAS from the *Dhammapada* discussed here are of universal relevance, and capable of generating significant insights. First,

> *Easily seen are the faults of others,*
> *Hard indeed to see are one's own;*
> *The faults of others you bring to light*
> *Like winnowing the chaff,*
> *But your own faults you cover up*
> *As the trickster conceals a losing throw.*

Here, our tendency to hide our faults is likened to the subterfuge of a cheat, because essentially we are being dishonest with ourselves. To acknowledge how we really are, however, is extremely difficult, particularly with regard to our faults, because our opinion of ourselves is always so wide of the mark – it is either too high or too low. The best way to get a clear and realistic picture of ourselves is to observe ourselves mindfully.

It isn't difficult for us to notice other people's faults as these so frequently annoy us, and in this negative state we are convinced that what we think is right, and that we are entitled to pass judgement. This makes us quick to criticize, and in doing so we forget that our thinking is based on our own opinions, which cannot be completely objective. In a sense, all our opinions are wrong, because they are rooted in our ego-illusion: 'I have, I want, I will; I believe, I know, I think.' On the relative level, these opinions of ours may be true, but relative truth can never be enough to completely satisfy us, because in the end it can only express the truth of one ego against that of another. One person believes this, another believes that; one does it this way, the other does it exactly the opposite way. Truth that is built around the notion of an ego cannot be the absolute and unadorned. At best, it reflects personal preferences. Relative truth can do no more than that.

From the point of view of absolute truth it is a very different picture. From this perspective, we begin to realize that the faults we are concerned with in others should be recognized with the same concern in ourselves. The faults of others are a reflection of our own, otherwise we wouldn't be able to recognize them. When we see someone being angry or showing off, we recognize these failings from our own experience of them in ourselves. We know how these emotional reactions come about and how they feel. By the same token, it is said that only a Buddha can recognize a Buddha, because only an Enlightened One knows about Enlightenment.

When we become aware that we are criticizing other people we should immediately realize that we are on the wrong track. Our criticism is unlikely to be of use; after all, who has ever changed through being carped at? Spreading negativity is always harmful, mostly to ourselves. We can also expect the other person to be annoyed at us, and if we react with anger and resentment, we can get into a vicious circle of ever more negativity, and possibly lose a friend.

So criticism is not helpful – but acknowledgement is. If, for example, we notice someone being unmindful, the right response would be, 'I wonder how mindful I am at the moment?' This is the only worthwhile response. If we observe something unskilful in someone, and want to criticize, we should remind ourselves that criticism is harmful to us.

By the time repeated criticism becomes a habit, we have carved ruts of negativity within ourselves. We probably all know someone who habitually criticizes, and we know how unpleasant it is to listen to them. Consequently, we must be on our guard against criticism, and avoid inflicting such an unpleasant habit on others. We should also be aware that every time we criticize we are gradually forming a habit.

Conversely, if we take the opportunity to observe what exactly is going on in the other person, we can make use of what we notice in their behaviour as a kind of mirror on ourselves. This is a very valuable mirror, because although it may not give us a view of our physical features, it does enable us to embark upon the much more difficult task of knowing ourselves. The task is difficult because not only do we lack awareness, but we prefer it that way – we prefer not to know the truth; we are anxious to avoid it because we fear it will be unpleasant.

Two of the eight worldly phenomena are involved here: praise and blame. Preoccupying ourselves with winning praise and avoiding blame are obviously a little absurd, but we don't ever really question them. In addition, they underlie our reluctance to take up any kind of self-analysis: we are afraid to find out things about ourselves for which we might have to accept blame. We prefer to wear blinkers and avoid an all-round look at ourselves.

The fear of blame may be dealt with using the formula 'acknowledge, don't blame, change'. The first step is to become aware of this fear of being rebuked, disagreement, and lack of support and appreciation.

The root of all fear is the fear of non-existence. Subliminally it is present in every one of us, and it can surge up in panic, simply because we do not want to incur blame. At the same time we are always ready to blame others, in the belief that this will not harm us. But we are mistaken; in giving way to negativity, it is we who suffer.

The fear of blame is the same as our fear of death, or our fear on behalf of our ego, our self-affirmation. Ultimately, it is the fear of not being here any more. Of course, when we anticipate blame, we are not afraid of actually disappearing on the spot, we are afraid of the disappearance of our self-esteem, which depends on the appreciation of others.

Clearly, this is completely crazy, yet most people are totally convinced by this scenario, some to the point of obsession, so that they are forever trying to please everyone. But how can we possibly hope to do this? We do not even know what another person's feelings and wishes are in the first place. But although we cannot make everything right for everyone, we can always try to do what is most skilful.

It is a fact of life that we all want acclamation and praise. Our actions are geared to this end, and if our desire is frustrated we become seized by a fear that prevents objectivity. In other words, we are afraid of criticism. To cast off this fear, we should begin by trying not to be so critical ourselves, understanding that whatever we do returns like a boomerang.

This first step towards insight into cause and effect – something observable everywhere in the universe – is insufficient to overcome all fear. The second step involves understanding the nature of fear. In our quest for affirmation from others we make ourselves the slaves of our environment. So long as this environment fails to match our expectations, or to permanently confirm how wonderful, intelligent, or beautiful we are, we will continue to be uncomfortable. Such an attitude makes life enormously difficult, and obstructs our progress towards self-knowledge.

Conversely, honest self-knowledge is essential in enabling us to let go, including letting go our fear of blame. We can only let go of that which we have fully recognized for ourselves, and it is quite unnecessary to transform our fear of blame into fear of self-knowledge; the fact that we are able to let go of self after we have understood it doesn't mean that we die. It means that self-centredness is no longer the dominant force in our life. Things need not revolve around how *we* see them all the time. Instead, we open up a space within for that which is universally true. We then understand that because there are faults in every aspect of conditioned existence, nothing perfect is to be found anywhere.

Just consider the fact of impermanence: all that has come into being must pass away, and nothing stays the same. If we try to hold on to an experience of something it slips away like sand through our fingers. The fundamental unreliability of things can of course become an occasion for blame, especially when other people let us down by not keeping an appointment or not completing a job properly.

No one would ever criticize a star in the sky when it becomes a supernova and fades away – we know that it would be pointless to offer such a reproach, since it just happens. But in reality this is the true nature of all things, and it is equally pointless to complain about the unreliability of everything else in the universe. All conditioned things are imperfect.

This is why it is worth while to look at ourselves without fear, and see what it is about other people that we don't like. Do we dislike their negativity? We should examine ourselves for negativity. Do we dislike their constant attention-seeking? Is it possible that we too have the same desire to be the centre of attention? In this way, we will get to know ourselves better and better.

We all know the fear that arises, again and again, in the course of this exercise: 'Maybe I am not quite as nice as I thought – and if I am not so nice, other people are going to disapprove of me.' I call this 'result-oriented thinking'; we stiffen up in fear against its threat, as if against the whip, and this can lead to a physical pain. We believe that everything has to be perfect, right in every way. But what is it that we expect to be right? In the universe, everything goes its own way, on and on. Rivers flow, and any attempt to stop them causes a flood. Life flows on; as each day comes to an end, a new day begins. Why do we not give ourselves to this flowing of things, and stop thinking about putting in its way all the things that have to be right?

This applies to our meditation as much as to anything else. Although we may be sitting quietly on our cushion, with no one saying anything or criticizing us, we still find we are putting pressure on ourselves and blocking our meditation. If we think our meditation has to be perfect we will be unable to meditate and encounter only anxiety.

It is pointless to expect to do everything perfectly; we can only give of our best. We are also much better off if we can give up the wish to be appreciated. Of course, if someone does offer us appreciation, gratitude, even joy, for what we have done, that is good – but a good thing for them.

We should also remember that we are constantly changing. Our powers and capabilities can be seen to fluctuate from one moment to the next. This also applies in meditation. Sometimes the mind may focus very quickly; on other occasions it may have to clear away so many thoughts that an hour has elapsed before we attain a degree of stillness. This ability or inability we tend to refer back to our 'self' – we take it on as our own – but why do we feel the need to do this? What is really happening is that the mind is constantly changing.

If we can see how everything changes in ourselves, it is reasonable to conclude that the same goes for everyone else. If someone behaves in a way unworthy of praise, we should appreciate that they will change, hopefully for the better. So in becoming more aware of impermanence – especially impermanence of bad behaviour – we will find it easier to let go of nit-picking and the urge to find fault.

As we have seen, what we resent most in others are those features that we like least in ourselves. We have also seen that if we take time once in a while to investigate and understand these tendencies, we can make the effort to overcome them. However, in the course of this process we are liable to dole out especially heavy criticism, because while the behaviour we observe may resemble our own, the people we criticize may not be making the effort towards purification that we are making. Such an attitude creates a lot of friction in relationships; it does not have to be explicit, but nevertheless we harbour feelings of disapproval and antipathy. Time and again we need to make a fresh effort to accept others and refrain from criticism. This is true even with respect to ourselves. We should not carp and cavil, but keep reminding ourselves of the formula, 'acknowledge, don't blame, change'.

This first part – getting a clear view of ourselves – is the most difficult. The second – not blaming – is not easy either, as the mind automatically responds negatively to any unpleasant feeling. All that we dislike in ourselves – everything we cannot accept and would like to change – produces unpleasant feelings and self-reproach, and the way towards self-knowledge can be lost sight of.

It is insight into impermanence that facilitates self-inquiry. When it becomes clear that everything we see is at that moment disappearing, it will be much easier to avoid falling into self-blame. Everything that comes will go and never return – and nothing that comes after will be quite the same, however similar it may seem. By investigating impermanence in this way we start to be able to accept ourselves and others more readily.

Recognizing the true nature of what we denounce in others helps us to a fresh view of ourselves. We free ourselves from what offends us not by turning away from the people with these faults, but by dropping the need to make others responsible for not being how we think they should be.

In this process we can recognize both impermanence and dukkha. Realizing that dukkha arises from our own negative reactions, which include the fear of criticism, will make it easier to refrain from criticizing others. We can clearly see that almost everyone knows the fear that derives from lack of support and affirmation, and that this type of dependence on people is extremely unpleasant.

How do we suppose that other people can ever have the right opinion of us? Have we not woken up to the fact that we are all trapped in an illusion that makes it impossible to have a truly objective opinion? This illusion is that we are all separate individuals and that we can have exclusively pleasant sense contacts if we are clever enough to arrange things in the right way.

Everyone lives under this illusion, which gives them a craving for existence and a fear of annihilation. How, then, is it possible for someone else to give us confirmation of our existence? All fears reflect this fear of annihilation. Fear is not limited to fear for our physical existence, but extends to our emotional existence, our self-affirmation. But if we become aware of this fear, we can also develop a deeper empathy with others, for all mankind has this craving for existence, which gives rise to the most severe dukkha.

This deeply-rooted fear is what stands in the way of perfect contentment on a basic human level, and once we begin to understand this correlation, we will stop searching for fulfilment in the wrong places. Instead, we will try to transcend the difficulties of the human condition caused by ego-illusion. First, however, we have to recognize that the fear of honest self-inquiry, together with the fear of being criticized by others and the corresponding urge to criticize them, are motivated by the need to bolster our self-affirmation. In condemning others we are making ourselves feel better. We will come closer to the truth if we admit that we all have weaknesses.

This recognition takes us a big step further towards insight into the fundamental insufficiency of existence on this human, conditioned, level. It is only once we have become aware of this insufficiency that we will experience an urgency to leave this level behind – not physically, of course, but in terms of letting go of our ego-illusion. The problems we have overcome will no longer trouble us, and we will gain insight into whatever other problems continue to cause us difficulties. We will be able to see that we haven't yet transcended those problems inasmuch as events can still disturb us. If, for example, we read bad news and instantly feel negativity welling up within us, we can assume that we have not yet lost our greed and hatred. There is a lot of destruction in the world, but irritation and condemnation only show that hatred is still deeply-rooted within.

We are all born with six roots – three good ones and three bad ones – which is why it is pointless to condemn ourselves or others. The only response that makes any sense is the recognition of these roots, and to commit ourselves to encouraging the good ones to flourish, so as gradually to attenuate the unwholesome.

The unwholesome roots are of course greed, hatred, and delusion (delusion in the sense of ego-illusion). But their opposites should be just as familiar to us. If we can see the three good roots – of generosity, unconditional love, and wisdom – in other people, we may draw the natural conclusion that they are present within us also. Actually, we do know perfectly well exactly when, where, and how to practise. Words and precepts are never enough on their own, but we already have sufficient wisdom within us to sense the truth when we hear it, and to know where it can be found.

> *Those who always find fault with others,*
> *Who criticize constantly,*
> *Their own cravings will grow,*
> *Far are they from the cessation of their desires.*

'Cessation of desires' is another term for perfect purification. It means that greed and hatred are no longer present, and when they have died away one is only a little short of complete Enlightenment. Until then, as these words of the Buddha make quite clear, there is a lot of inner work to be done, for as long as we criticize we will be unaware of our real motives and unable to work on them.

These motives are principally the two roots of greed and hatred. Both spring from delusion, or ignorance, from the illusion that leads us to believe that there really is 'someone'. On the relative level it is certainly true that we sit here on our cushion, but the absolute truth is quite different. Inasmuch as we live according to relative truth, as a 'me' that exists in relation to 'you', we experience ourselves as separate from others, and want to protect and build walls around ourselves. To do this we draw on these motives, and they are strengthened whenever we are negative.

This is what makes it is so important to maintain mindful observation of our emotional reactions – to be mindful of them again and again, as they occur, even if we cannot let go of them. Once we notice those reactions we will notice also how much restlessness they stir up, and therefore how inimical they are to the calmness we need for meditation. In everyday life, it is not easy to notice the difference between a calm mind and a restless mind, but meditation over a longer period makes this contrast more apparent. We see that our reactions do not consist only of criticism; their roots can be traced back to desire, to aversion, and to fear.

According to the Buddha, our cravings grow when we look at the faults of others and indulge in negative reactions, because this re-inforces our separateness, which in turn leads to an even more entrenched ego-illusion. Conversely, our relationships can also help us to a deeper insight if we realize that others are subject to the same laws of impermanence, suffering, and unsatisfactoriness as we are. In fact, we should regard relationships with other people as occasions for learning, and if we make this use of them, we will benefit from a first-rate educational system. Indeed, we can view our life as a whole as a continuous opportunity to learn. All relationships can be a measure of our training in love and compassion, and an excellent opportunity to get to know ourselves.

If we dismiss or condemn someone, we are restless inside. The moment we let go of this feeling of censoriousness, peace returns. Letting go is not easy, but there are many small insights that can help us on the way towards it, for example, the insight that we ourselves have created this restlessness, and that it harms us.

If we keep reflecting on impermanence and dukkha, we start to understand that the whole universe is subject to them. Everything is in a constant process of dissolution, of passing away and arising anew. It is because of this uninterrupted movement of everything that nothing can be entirely satisfying. Once we recognize the fact of impermanence in all things, we no longer suffer from it. We are, after all, one of a community of six billion people, each of whom experiences exactly the same fact of life.

We can apply the general principles of impermanence and dukkha to any situation. This is the next step on the path towards insight, that we should observe these characteristics in everything we lay our eyes on. We will then see that nothing is perfectly satisfying, that everything is impermanent. In making this survey, no exceptions can be made. Everything has to be included. We cannot say, 'I have the experience of dukkha, but that person who caused me so much dukkha is a good-for-nothing.' In fact, he experiences as much dukkha as us. So gradually, in this way, we develop a feeling that the world is a totality, that it does not merely consist of individual phenomena.

Each time we react with fear, the sum total of fear in the world is increased. Each time we harbour negativity, disapproval, or blame, the sum total of negativity is increased. Conversely, if we understand impermanence and dukkha, this insight deepens the sum total of wisdom in the world. If we see clearly that each individual bears a responsibility for the totality, we will be more ready to dwell at a level on which we no longer see everything as separate.

Each good deed adds to the good in the world, because we are the world. Our feelings, thoughts, words, and actions are constituents of the world. On this basis, it is simply short-sighted to criticize; to do so is to overlook the fundamental characteristics or 'marks' of existence, which are that it is impermanent, insubstantial, and imbued with dukkha. The longer we meditate, and the more deeply we absorb and reflect on the universal truths of the Dhamma, the easier it will be to be mindful of these marks of existence and apply them to everyday life.

On the level of absolute truth there are no separate entities, everything is manifestation, but on the relative level everyone bears responsibility for the manifestation of the good. Fear is a characteristic that can be traced back to our desire to retain an essentially fixed and separate nature as individuals, and for life to be pleasant all the time. Both these desires are unrealistic: we cannot possibly stay here for ever and things cannot possibly be pleasant all the time, so fear arises in relation to both these aims and blocks our path. Fear can be a very powerful emotion. It is said that 'the fear of death is worse than death'. Likewise, such an emotion disables any attempt to sustain real insight. Nearly every meditator has known the fear that can arise during concentration, when suddenly their ego-affirmation goes into temporary abeyance.

Once we have overcome this fear, the next step is to realize that we have been chasing the impossible. Then the wish, indeed the urge, to transcend this ordinary human level of existence will develop. The fear that arises in the course of this process needs to be relinquished not once but many times, whenever we are assailed by the fear that our ego is under threat. It is essentially the same fear as when we are being blamed, or being denied the ego-confirmation we crave. There are many different names for fear, but it is basically the fear of non-existence.

The most effective antidote to our tendency to find faults in ourselves and others is to witness the truth of impermanence and dukkha. It is not really enough to tell ourselves, 'I should not find fault.' We have probably known this for a long time. The trouble is that we are so often attracted to the things we should not be. In this respect, only an attitude of engagement with insight, the main purpose of meditation, can help us.

Meditation is supposed to allow us to experience ourselves more deeply, which is why it should be backed up by contemplation and reflection, in order to increase our self-awareness. What degree of fear do we harbour in ourselves; how much do we fear losing ourselves? This kind of inquiry takes us closer to the truth. The crucial issue here is not whether we are able to let go of our fear immediately, but whether we can gain new insights through this examination of ourselves.

We can learn many things from the faults of others. Above all, we can get to know a lot about ourselves; when we do, we will feel a sense of connection, of solidarity with others, as though they are our brothers and sisters. Conversely, for as long as we keep separating ourselves and emphasizing our personal differences, our craving, greed, and hatred will grow even stronger.

Ugga, the royal minister, went to see the Exalted One.
Upon arrival he greeted him respectfully, and sitting down
beside him spoke to the Exalted One in these words: 'It is
wonderful, it is astonishing, how rich and wealthy, how
richly endowed this Migāra is, the grandson of Rohaṇa.'

'How rich may he be, this Migāra, Rohaṇa's grandson?'
asked the Buddha.

'Ten million in gold, oh Lord, not to speak of the silver.'

'Certainly, Ugga, it is not to be denied that this is a
treasure,' said the Buddha, 'but this treasure is threatened
by fire, water, princes, thieves, and undesirable heirs. There
are seven treasures which are not threatened in such a way.
What are they? The treasure of faith and confidence, the
treasure of ethical conduct, the treasure of shame, the
treasure of fear of blame, the treasure of knowledge, the
treasure of generosity, and the treasure of wisdom. These
seven treasures are not exposed to the danger of fire, water,
princes, thieves, or undesirable heirs.'

Aṅguttara-Nikāya vii.7

5

Two Kinds of Treasure

THE DISCOURSE called 'Two Kinds of Treasure' is taken from the
Aṅguttara-Nikāya, the 'Basket of Gradual Sayings' or 'Collection of
Numerical Discourses'. The *suttas* in the *Aṅguttara-Nikāya* are
grouped according to the number of items discussed, so in the first
volume all the discourses deal with one issue, in the second with two,
and so on. This discourse looks at a sevenfold issue, and is particularly relevant to us because it contrasts the worldly life with the
spiritual life, and clearly differentiates between these two possible
directions for one's life, and the two varieties of treasure one may
accumulate. This is not to say that either of these aspects is to be
despised. For one thing, contempt is a negative state of mind. For
another, it is a grave misconception to believe that the everyday
world has lost all value once we have embarked on the path of
spiritual development; we all continue to depend on the world for
the means to continue our practice.

All religions remind us that everything we achieve in our worldly
life will be lost, and most people remain aware of this subconsciously,
but tend to forget it when they start to pile up worldly treasure. The
dangers the Buddha mentions are with us still, though sometimes in
different forms: instead of princes we have the Inland Revenue and
job insecurity, while thieves are as prevalent as ever, and fire and
water and other natural and man-made disasters threaten us as they
have always done.

One of the many fears all human beings have to live with is the
greater or lesser fear of losing material possessions. People say, 'What

will happen to me when I'm old?' or 'The economic situation seems to be getting worse and worse – where is it all going to end?' The inner restlessness these fears provoke cannot be overcome until we come to recognize that the inner treasure mentioned here is much more valuable than anything we might fear losing – and that external benefits will automatically follow upon the possession of this inner treasure anyway. But few people believe this; they do not have the deep level of self-confidence that faith requires.

The majority of us rely on external wealth – material possessions such as property and money – and the fear of loss drives us to amass more and more of it. We rarely set any limit on what we want, or believe we have enough. The limit is often set only by external factors. Either we can earn no more or we reach the limit of our abilities, or we reach some sort of stagnation brought about by other factors. If we have talent, ideas, and fantasies, we often think our possessions are inadequate. A substantial material benefit such as an inheritance falls into the lap of very few people. Even then, one has to work to maintain the privileges and wealth one has earned or inherited – hence the warning in the discourse that wealth may be lost by heirs, that is, by those who fritter everything away. It requires an effort just to enjoy wealth properly.

Migāra is mentioned quite a few times in the Pāli Canon. He comes from a well-to-do family, having inherited his riches from his grand-father, Rohana, who first accumulated it. The Buddha does not deny that this is a treasure. He does not say, 'Material wealth is bad.' But he does point out that it is vulnerable and unreliable. If someone owns a fortune and uses it prudently, all well and good, but far greater treasure lies to hand, we are told, in a happiness that is not dependent on wealth, but on one's inner life.

The very rich in society are constantly under pressure, always harassed in the struggle to hang on to their wealth and protect it, and on this level there can be no peace whatsoever. But it is hardly any better on the level of the ordinary working person, who is so busy earning money that they have no time or energy to accumulate spiritual treasures. Our energies are naturally limited, and if we want to pursue a spiritual path we will need to make room for that in our everyday life. It's well worth taking a look at our material needs in order to see if there is something we can perhaps relinquish. The energy made available can be deployed to develop our inner treasure.

The word 'treasure' is very appropriate in this context. Our inner life can be a world of chaos and a source of pain. However, it can be a world of jewelled beauty and harmony, and a rich source of joy to be shared with others, a radiant happiness.

As much commitment is required for our inner work as for our mundane occupations, and we have to maintain a wise balance between the two. It is of course vital to keep our mundane affairs in order, to take care of our physical body and our environment. But all too often the external circumstances we create do not contribute to a happy inner life. Indeed, a purely materialistic orientation, however successful in its own terms, can be a real obstacle to our deeper needs. We can enjoy a happy inner life only if we take the trouble to sort out our inner experience of ourselves, and make space for the accumulation of inner treasure, the second kind of treasure to which the title of the sutta refers.

Faith and Confidence

The first of these inner treasures the Buddha refers to is faith and confidence. Most people need an object for their faith, and this object will often be a person or persons, albeit as imperfect as they are themselves. On the basis of this kind of mundane rather than spiritual investment of faith, disappointments are inevitable.

We can have faith only in what we love. We need an ideal that we can love, but also one that clearly shows us there is something beyond the mundane world. We are all only too familiar with the inherently dualistic values of the market place: as we go about buying and selling, we want to get back something equivalent to what we have paid out. But because the attitude we bring to the market place is always to do with the me–you mind set, thus separating us from other people, we constantly feel threatened, never quite safe. We may think we can buy security, but the *feeling* of safety cannot be bought. At some stage we need to recognize that this market-place thinking, the usual way of the world, can be the basis only for bare survival, and that as human beings we are able to transcend this level of existence. If we can recognize that we have within us the potential to realize a higher ideal, an ideal that we can love and trust, we will also have the confidence to develop the inner qualities to enable us to realize that potential.

It is impossible to find inner peace and happiness in mundane existence. We know outward peace as long as there is no war, and external happiness as long as we have pleasant sense contacts. But enjoyable sense experience is by its nature brief, and needs renewing again and again. The rich treasure of our inner life, by contrast, we carry within us all the time. Its nature is such that, whoever we are, it offers us something to work with all the time; it is also such that no one has the same inner life as anyone else. Once we begin to see this, inner riches replace the wealth of the outside world as the main focus of our interest.

Faith and confidence involve learning to love the path of spiritual evolution, to trust in it, to discover it within ourselves. They involve the realization that we can give ourselves completely to that path, reorient ourselves completely in that direction. They are also essentially, of course, inner qualities, and they refer to our potential for inner growth. So whatever adjustments we may have to make in order to give priority to spiritual values over our everyday lives, they do not necessarily include giving up our job or selling our house. Growth takes place within.

Faith and confidence involve a willingness to give ourselves totally. Without this dedication there can be no meditative concentration; in meditation we will continue to hang on to our thinking process as the last system of support for the self. Dedication to a spiritual ideal, to the highest truth, to transcending the human predicament, is only possible with faith and confidence. In meditation it should be easy to trust one's own breath – after all, we have known it for decades. Why is giving oneself up to one's own breath still so difficult? We are scared to give up thinking because when we do not think, we cannot perceive our own existence.

Faith, and above all faith in the seven treasures, opens the door to the spiritual life, for it shows us there is something higher. Everyone carries this treasure within themselves. Time and again it gets buried under our negative thinking, our greed, and our aversion – all the rubble, so to speak. But we can clear away the rubble and open this door through meditation, and thereby unfold new layers of the mind, one of which is the love expressed through faith and confidence. Whilst both intellect and heart are needed, faith and confidence is largely a matter of the heart.

If we are unable to put trust and confidence in something, our heart cannot be engaged. We will find ourselves limping along, as it were, on the one foot of our intellect, and not getting very far. The intellect has the ability to understand, but only the heart can experience, and the teaching of the Buddha is there to be experienced, not just understood. Faith engages the heart's potential where our views and opinions are no longer important. We have confidence in an *ideal*. We don't need to find a name for it, we may not even know what it is, but deep down we know there is something higher, something that goes beyond our human problems. Most of us, when we look within, discover a longing for that inexpressible something, and we frequently take a number of diversions and wrong turnings while searching for it, before we realize that it can be found only within ourselves.

Ethical Conduct

Ethical conduct is the second treasure, and is a reference to the five precepts. These provide a fundamental basis for a harmonious life. If we live such a life day by day, we will not get into the kind of trouble that can cripple our spiritual practice.

The first precept is about not killing living beings. This means all beings, irrespective of how large or small they are. The precept is meant to attenuate and unearth the root of hatred in us, with a view eventually to eliminating all negativity towards anything whatsoever. This is not to say we will be unable to distinguish between good and bad. We will recognize good and bad, but we will understand that it is not our job to judge people. Our duty is nothing other than to achieve freedom by the eradication of all impurities.

The function of this precept is not only to weaken our hatred, but at the same time to develop unconditional love. The ideas we have about love are always bound up with difficulties – not only because we get attached, but also because they get confused with the market-place mentality; we want something in return for what we give. This kind of thinking is utterly mistaken: the nature of love is to liberate, not to bind, and it has no room for fear. Love has only one purpose: to give, and over time we will understand this, that love is a quality of the heart that depends not on its recipient, but on our ability to give it out regardless. From the standpoint of love, the fact that the recipient is one person rather than another is incidental. It doesn't in fact matter whether the love is being noticed or even wanted – or indeed whether anyone is there to receive it at all.

If intelligence is the faculty of the intellect, love is the faculty of the heart. But while a large number of institutions promote intellectual training, we have no educational establishments where the development of qualities of the heart is taught. We expect love to just come naturally. But nothing happens automatically; even autonomous processes like breathing depend on the appropriate conditions for support. This idea that love can be left to sort itself out is a fiction from the imagination, and causes nothing but trouble. However, we can employ the love we are familiar with as a seedbed, and try to generate an experience of unconditional love out of that experience of conditioned love. In doing so, we are also working to reduce our hatred, the word 'hatred' here being a label for all our negativity, together with the excuses and justifications with which we defend it.

The teachings of the Buddha should not be taken as psychological theory, or psychotherapy, nor as philosophical treatise, but as practical instruction that leads to inner happiness and peace. As long as we make ourselves dependent on external conditions or on other people, we are not free. We are more like slaves, inasmuch as we rely on things working out as planned. We can only be free from this kind of constraint when we have purified ourselves and developed the heart's capacities to such an extent that they become self-supporting. This independence is the starting point for freedom, where we get a glimpse of what it means to be truly free.

Everyone has the potential to love, but most people develop it to such a limited extent that it is dependent on their being found lovable, or having their love reciprocated. Some people even think they have no such potential. In fact, everyone has this faculty to love, if they know how to develop it. While it is of course much easier to sense the feeling of love when face to face with a lovable and attractive person, that feeling is one of dependence, and the Buddha's teaching is that only independence in this respect will release us finally from dukkha, from grief.

The second precept is about not taking the not given. Its positive counterpart, liberality or open-handed generosity, figures separately as another of the seven treasures later on. The quotation 'it is more blessed to give than to receive,' is well known, but who actually behaves as if it were true? Who actually follows maxims like this in their everyday life? Usually we don't give them a second thought, because our knowledge and our action are poles apart. Although we may have theoretical knowledge, we do not acknowledge that we hardly ever apply it. Useful as knowledge is – and it, too, counts as one of the seven treasures – true practice begins only when we are able to make these treasures our own. We have to go to work every day in order to earn our living, and the same is true on the spiritual level. We have to work with our experience of ourselves day after day in order to discover these inner treasures.

The third precept is about abstention from sexual misconduct. Its positive counterparts are fidelity, responsibility, and reliability – including fidelity towards friends and family. In general terms this involves conducting ourselves in such a way that no one gets hurt emotionally, and certainly not physically. This principle of not harming anyone is based on the cultivation of love, but as with the second precept, it aims also at the renunciation of craving – in the sense of anything connected with our wishing and wanting. Wanting to possess is what leads us into extra difficulties and at the same time locks us in a state of restlessness. Once we want something, it is never enough to get it. We become attached to it, that is, we want to continue to have it or to have it again, which is an endless waste of energy. Craving is more difficult to recognize than hatred, but equally harmful.

When we condemn something, or recoil from something or resist it, we can – if we pay careful attention – notice an unmistakably unpleasant feeling. Craving, however, promises satisfaction, since we imagine that once our wishes are fulfilled, everything will be fine. At some point we realize that whatever it was we had our eye on was not the right thing after all, not the thing that gives us ultimate satisfaction, and our desire moves on to the next object. Thus we are trapped in an ever-rolling restlessness, a continuing anxiety as to whether we will get what we want and whether we will be able to hold on to it. When the inevitable happens and we lose it again, the circle of desire starts afresh.

In order to recognize this pattern we need a degree of mindfulness. These treasures can be realized only if we pay attention to ourselves. Mindfulness is not enumerated as one of the seven treasures, but it is a necessary precondition for the spiritual path. Without introspection we cannot discover the wealth within.

The next precept is about untruthful and harsh speech. This includes any kind of speech that might cause harm, that condemns something in an unpleasant way, expresses ill will, or amounts to gossip or useless chatter. Its positive counterpart is the effort to purify one's thoughts so that our speech is truthful and harmonious. The essential precondition for this, again, is mindfulness of the content of our thoughts. When we start meditating we realize very soon that the mind invents any number of fantasies that are entirely insubstantial, sometimes outright absurd, and neither helpful nor contributive to anything – just a lot of unwanted ideas and fantasies. Recognition of this will make it much easier to discredit the unwholesome thoughts in our everyday life, and turn them into wholesome ones. If we want to take the spiritual path, the practice of mindfulness is a most useful starting point.

The Buddha's teaching of the 'four right efforts' can be most easily remembered as a concise formula: 'avoid, overcome, develop, sustain' – but putting them into practice is of course quite another thing. First of all, it means making sure that unwholesome thoughts don't get the chance to arise. If they are already there, it means getting the better of them, that is, replacing them with positive ones. If positive thoughts have not yet arisen, it means producing them. And, fourthly, if positive thoughts are already present, it means maintaining them.

When we start to apply the four right efforts we no longer allow our thoughts to fool around as usual. We no longer really trust our thoughts, and we check carefully whether they are wholesome or unwholesome, skilful or unskilful. This is difficult at first, but after a time it comes more naturally, and it becomes clearer that it is possible to replace unwholesome thoughts with wholesome ones, resulting in a state of tranquillity.

Negative, unwholesome emotions give rise to inner restlessness and lethargy, and if we are interested in a spiritual and well-balanced life it is vital to investigate our mental states in order to unearth them, otherwise our motivation, even on a spiritual level, amounts to no more than fancies and high hopes. As ever, it is purification that can help us sort out our inner chaos.

Because speech is such a spontaneous process we are not generally aware that we put into words only what we have already thought, so a precondition for observation of the fourth precept is mindful observation of our thoughts and our general behaviour.

The fifth precept is about not taking alcohol and drugs, as they only add to the mind's confusion. In its positive form it is about practising mindfulness in daily life. By constantly observing ourselves we get to know ourselves more and more deeply, and eventually we will be able to see through to the absolute truth of existence. We have many fanciful ideas about who we are – ideas that maintain the illusion that we are someone special, fictions that we constantly renew for the sake of self-confirmation. If we look deeply, however, we will recognize who we really are.

Mindfulness in daily life starts with observation of our physical movements, feelings, moods, and thoughts. Our awareness easily slips, but once we notice this we can become mindful again. It is a matter of learning how to be careful with the mind, realizing that just as we learn to take care of our body – we don't want to have an accident, or even get scratched – so we need to think, speak, and act carefully, so that the mind is not harmed.

Ethical conduct is a very important and profound part of our inner treasure. Not only do we recognize standards by which we can observe and take care of ourselves, but ethical practice also opens the possibility for the skilful development of the next two treasures, shame or decency, and fear of blame by the wise.

Shame

Shame and fear of blame by the wise are called the guardians of the world, because a sense of decency and the fear of disapproval by good people prevents us doing evil. If basic decency is lost, as happens in war and under dictatorships, the result is a moral chaos that infects the minds and hearts of the people as a whole – though this does not take away the responsibility for each individual, even in such situations, to preserve their conscience. So shame is a guardian that saves both the world and the individual from the worst excesses of moral breakdown.

None of us can live without help. Once in a while it is worth considering: 'Where does my food come from? Who built my home? Who produced my clothes? How does my mail reach me? How do I feel being part of a team?' From our answers we can see that nobody can live completely on their own. Do we not all breathe the same air? Do we not all depend on the same natural world around us?

It works the other way too, of course. If we say that everyone who does something bad carries this blemish into the world and pollutes the environment, we are referring to the same connectedness of all things. We need only call to mind any event that has taken a toll on human lives. The environment can be polluted by the thoughts of one person or group of people in such a way that millions have to suffer; just think of the last world war.

However, the forces of goodness have the same potential as the forces of evil, and with the treasure of shame we can strive to better ourselves and exert an opposing influence on the pollution. Since we do not live in isolation, each of us bears a responsibility to foster and maintain the good by our thoughts and actions. Evil may be able to overwhelm the world in various ways and at various times, but goodness holds its ground, otherwise we would have perished long ago. There are always enough people who do good.

Our sense of decency protects us and the world from the unwholesome. Nobody who wants to be decent goes out with a dirty face and dirty clothes. If they did, they would certainly do something about it as soon as they noticed – they'd run back to wash and change. We ought to be just as ashamed of unwholesome, negative thoughts, and do something about them just as quickly.

If we can realize through mindfulness that nobody exists separately, we will certainly find it easier to take on responsibility for the world. We each have an important part to play in the complex chains of events that determine the way the world operates. Observance of the five precepts will naturally help us conduct ourselves so that we need feel no shame or regret. Instead, we will enjoy knowing that we have done our best.

In another discourse, the freedom from regret which is the result of ethical conduct is mentioned as one of the conditions for access to the entire spiritual path. We will be free from regret when we have purified our thoughts and words. If we do behave unskilfully, it is certainly appropriate to feel remorse; we will not become free of regret by being shameless. On the other hand, it is extremely unskilful to fret over the past. We have to remind ourselves that the person who acted wrongly in the past is not the one who now experiences remorse – had we been aware as we are now, we would not have acted so unskilfully. Instead of crying over it, we should forgive the person we used to be, and start afresh. Every day brings a new beginning. Burdening ourselves with self-reproach will only make it more difficult to find our feet on the spiritual path.

Fear of Blame, or Concern for Wise Opinion

Along with the treasure of shame or decency goes the fear of blame by the wise. This fear of blame is a healthy fear: fear of doing something that is not right. It is entirely justified because we are constantly tempted to allow hatred or craving to surface without appreciating the consequences of giving way to them. This tendency to lapse into negativity may be so subtle that we will be unaware of it and believe our intentions to be acceptable. Hence along with shame comes an awareness of the need to practise mindfulness.

The fear of doing wrong also arises when we realize we are subject to the law of karma. Everyone knows the quotation from the New Testament: 'whatsoever a man soweth, that shall he also reap,' but do people really understand what this means in practice? Karma, the explanation of conditionality on the ethical plane, provides the foundation of the Buddha's teaching. Fear of unskilful actions is based on the understanding that we and no one else will reap their fruit. We should not hide from shame and blame; they are our protectors and prevent us getting into trouble.

No amount of provocation excuses unskilful actions. Difficult situations should be the incentive for our practice. Suppose we are angry with someone: this anger mostly harms ourselves rather than the person with whom we are angry – and such is the case with all negative thinking, whether arrogance, jealousy, envy, or the apportioning of blame. But it can harm the other person if they react with such feelings themselves, in which case they, too, create bad karma. It is even possible to cause negativity in others without realizing it. The Buddha said, 'Karma, O monks, mark my words, comprises the intentions,' but the spiritual path requires first of all taking responsibility for our thoughts, words, and actions. If we don't lock our car, we are giving others the opportunity to steal, and the same is true of the spiritual life: we should avoid giving others the opportunity to create bad karma.

Knowledge

The next treasure is knowledge. The Buddha has left us a legacy that can lead us to perfect peace and happiness, but before we can set out on this path we need information about it. We need to know the methods and explanations taught by the Buddha. Unfortunately, we already have so much information in our heads that it is difficult to add fresh material. Moreover, we immediately compare new information with what we know already, and judge whether it matches. This comparison and evaluation, based on our own opinions, doesn't really get us anywhere. Instead, we should place some trust in the teaching, try it out, and see how it affects us. If the result is negative we can look for another way, but it is no good drawing comparisons on a purely intellectual level, as in books. Such comparison is only valid and useful when the entire path has been followed to its very end. It is only from the standpoint of Enlightenment and ultimate freedom that one can see how other paths can lead to the goal. Until then, the acquisition of new information is merely intellectual.

Knowledge drawn from the discourses of the Buddha, once it has been inwardly absorbed, can be put into practice immediately, assuming we can remember it. Our mind is usually so busy with mundane business that it completely forgets about spiritual work, but it is in the course of our daily life that we need to train the mind. A good memory helps, and it helps to write things down – for example, 'avoid, overcome, develop, sustain' – and post them up. Whenever we glance at those words we will be reminded to avoid and overcome the unwholesome, and to develop and sustain the wholesome. It is also a good idea, of course, to listen to talks and take notes, until everything is so rooted in the mind that we can understand the teaching and follow it effectively.

Generosity

The penultimate treasure, generosity, complements the second precept: not to take what is not given. Generosity – giving without thought of return – is often placed by the Buddha at the top of the list of virtues. Its opposite is ego-centredness, which manifests in our desire to keep things to ourselves and our discomfort if someone wants to take them away. This kind of addiction to ourselves is the root of all our problems: if there were no ego, who would have a problem? So all the Buddha's teaching is directed towards recognizing the illusion created by the importance we accord ourselves in the form of the ego. By developing open-handed generosity we bring about the surrender of ego-centredness.

The practice we are talking about involves much more than the reduction of egocentric behaviour. A generous person does not wait until a gift is expected of them, such as a special occasion, or being asked for something, before they think of giving. In a society like ours, in which most people have more than they need, we should not find it difficult to find material things to give away – though by the same token it is also difficult to make a real difference to others in terms of material gifts. In this sutta the Buddha says that our only justification for maintaining wealth is the participation of others. Of course, it is up to the individual how to manage this and how much to give, but such sharing should make a real difference: it should be more than just almsgiving. Even if we have no wealth, we have many other things we can give: our time, our talents, our love, our compassionate listening. Our energy is of at least as much benefit to others as financial support.

According to the Buddha, there is another consideration: that the purity of the recipient purifies what has been given. Generosity should be appropriate, and demonstrate an awareness of the recipient and their needs. It is easy for common sense to give way to pity, and pity is not, strictly speaking, a positive or pure emotion.

We can give out of compassion, generosity, or the desire to create good karma, but true generosity stems from the insight that we are all part of the same reality, all manifestations of existence. This is difficult to realize because of the illusion that we are all separate, but in reality there is nothing that is separate from anything else. In simple terms, if we make one person happy we will increase the world's happiness. We all have ability – indeed, the responsibility – to spread happiness.

Furthermore, generosity should be joyful. Some people cause a lot of resentment with the pompous demeanour, ideas, and opinions they insist on thrusting down everyone's throat. But such people can usually be helped on to the right path by reminding them that the skilful is intimately connected with the joyful. We all need incentives to impel us in the direction of the good; it does not, unfortunately, develop automatically. Everyone is born with three positive roots and three negative roots, all of which manifest in one way or another, and we need constantly to make an effort to strengthen the positive ones rather than the negative ones. The primary negative root is delusion, in the sense of being under the spell of our ego-illusion in our belief that 'I am someone'. This is the root from which the other two roots, greed and hatred, arise. The three positive roots are the ability to be wise, to love, and to be generous.

Through giving away outward treasures we experience the inner treasure of generosity. Indeed, our effort in practising all seven treasures produces so many positive results that the inner treasure becomes far more valuable than any mundane treasure. Once we have fully experienced this wealth we can never lose our inner joy, whereas even the richest man cannot continue the pleasure of studying his accounts – he will more likely become worried by the performance of some of his shares. But we can accumulate inner treasure within ourselves and at the same time give them away. They cannot be taken from us. Perhaps the best thing we can give is the clear sense of joy that spiritual work brings, which is more likely than anything else to encourage others to pursue it for themselves.

Being at the top of the list of virtues, generosity opens the gates, so to speak. When we truly give we open ourselves to others; we want nothing for ourselves. The key phrase is 'letting go'; in fact, letting go is the key to the spiritual path in general, as well as to meditation in particular. The views we have accumulated, and our insistence on holding on to them, are what prevent us from recognizing the truth, and the stirrings of greed and hatred are what make it so difficult to find the space of perfect happiness that exists within.

Wisdom
The last of the seven treasures is wisdom, in the sense of the opposite of delusion. It denotes understood experience, wisdom experienced and felt in the heart. To understand what we experience, we need knowledge about the spiritual path and the teaching that describes it. We learn that through the cultivation of awareness we can experience the bliss and tranquillity of concentration – by way of recognizing greed, hatred, and illusion within us and trying to remove them.

Understood experience, then, is the first step to wisdom, as both experience and understanding are necessary on the spiritual path. The acquisition of knowledge is not difficult. We constantly acquire knowledge, from kindergarten to university, in order to make our way through the world of work and business, but we do not thereby come any closer to wisdom. Our knowledge of the spiritual path needs to be put into practice in our day-to-day thinking, discussion, and action. We experience and understand the path if we abstain from our customary rejection of everything we don't like and grasping at everything that pleases us. Only thus will we become aware of our unwholesome tendencies, and on that basis try to transform them so that they no longer stand in our way. It is ego-centredness that blocks the spiritual path: I want, I will, I must, I can, I should, I want to get rid of. Dropping this fixation in order to become a neutral observer of one's inner life, and then purifying the unwholesome, is the spiritual path that generates wisdom.

Reading and understanding open doors, but they don't give us the experience. Understanding is a process of the mind; experience a process of the heart. If the two don't come together, we are only half way there.

If both heart and head are involved we can develop a new view of the world and of ourselves, no longer experiencing the world from the narrow viewpoint of our ego, but seeing it as a whole. If we take the subject of suffering, or dukkha, for example, our natural tendency is to resist it – and the more opposed we are to something, the more painful it will become. But when we understand that suffering is universal, we drop our resistance to it. As a result, as we develop compassion for ourselves and all other beings, we no longer suffer in that way.

This process can only be understood through regular daily practice. If we want to establish our lives on a truly spiritual foundation we have to practise mindfulness every day to enable the arising of 'understood experience'. This may seem difficult at first, because it is new and unfamiliar, but once we have practised it for a while it will become a matter of course to live mindfully. After all, such mindfulness also protects us from bad karma.

At the end of the discourse, this concluding stanza encapsulates all seven treasures:

Whoever lives ethically, with confidence and faith,
With fear of blame and conscientiousness,
Trained in liberality and knowledge,
With wisdom as the seventh treasure –
Whoever has found these treasures,
Be it man or woman,

They are rightly regarded as wealthy ones,
Not in vain have they lived.
That is why the wise ones should
Practise confidence and ethics,
Insight also, and faith,
Mindful of the Buddha's teaching.

There are five methods for conquering anger and resentment. They permit the eradication of every trace of anger or resentment. What are they? If anger arises, this is what should be done: cultivate loving-kindness, cultivate compassion, cultivate equanimity.... Do not pay attention, do not take heed of that person. If resentment arises, one should call to mind the law of ownership of one's actions, namely: 'The owner of his actions is he, this venerable one, he is heir to his actions, he is born out of his actions, he is tied to them, finds refuge in them, and what right and wrong he has done will be his heritage.'

Aṅguttara-Nikāya v.161

6

Five Ways to Overcome Anger and Resentment

ANYONE WHO HAS EXPERIENCED anger and resentment knows how unpleasant they are. Fortunately, the Buddha provided clear instructions on how to let go of anger and live in a way that will defend us from it, and he illustrated his message with parables to help us remember the instructions.

We all know how unpleasant anger is, but we find it difficult to let it go, and this is where the Buddha's practical advice can be very useful. The first and shorter discourse on the subject is entitled 'Five ways to overcome anger and resentment', and reads as follows:

> *There are five methods for conquering anger and resentment. They permit the eradication of every trace of anger or resentment. What are they? If anger arises, this is what should be done: cultivate loving-kindness, cultivate compassion, cultivate equanimity.*

But how can we cultivate such feelings in the very moment we feel angry? After all, love, compassion, and equanimity are three of the four highest emotions. The fourth, sympathetic joy, is not mentioned here perhaps because rejoicing in the merit of someone with whom we have just become angry is too much to ask, but if we cannot manage any of these three there is a fourth way, and that is:

> *Do not pay attention, do not take heed of that person.*

If we realize and accept that in certain situations we cannot handle our feelings, that we cannot overcome our anger and resentment, and that we are only harming ourselves, we can at least try to take our mind off it. We can turn away from this person and do something else until the anger and resentment has subsided a little, or the situation has changed sufficiently for us to be able to practise loving-kindness and compassion again.

On another occasion the Buddha offered the following example: 'We see a friend on the other side of the road, but we do not walk over to him, shake his hand, and ask how he is; instead, we act as though we had not seen him.' We stay on our side of the road because we know that meeting him would agitate us.

The fifth method is especially important:

> *If resentment arises, one should call to mind the law of*
> *ownership of one's actions, namely: 'The owner of his*
> *actions is he, this venerable one, he is heir to his actions, he*
> *is born out of his actions, he is tied to them, finds refuge in*
> *them, and what right and wrong he has done will be his*
> *heritage.'*

By owning one's actions is meant owning one's karma. This way of looking at karma – as a possession – is a common one, but it can give us a tremendously helpful perspective. If we get angry with someone because they have done something bad, we should remind ourselves that every person inherits the result of their intentions. The law of cause and effect is at work in the universe as well as in every individual. Intentional actions will have effects, and it is impossible to avoid them. Nevertheless, two people who perform the same action may yet experience very different results.

The Buddha explains this with a metaphor: 'If you put a teaspoon of salt into a cup of water, the water will be undrinkable. Yet if you sprinkle a teaspoon of salt in the Ganges, the water of the river will not change even a little.' The cup of water – as against the river – symbolizes a limited accumulation of skilful deeds: if we commit an unskilful deed on top of a mere cupful of skilful deeds, we can expect to reap serious trouble. If, however, we have a whole river-full of skilful deeds behind us, then one unskilful action may have no noticable effect at all. As we do not know what other people have done and thought in the past, whether in this life and in past lives, there is no way we can determine anyone else's karma. What we can see within ourselves, however, is that everyone harvests the fruit of their own actions.

If someone behaves badly, and we are thereby disadvantaged or harmed, we easily become angry. In that moment it is very important to remember that everyone makes their own way in life and creates their own pattern of cause and effect. How we are today is still very much the result of our intentions. Without the intention to find out about the Buddha's teaching – and many people have no interest in it – nobody would be reading this book. So taking sufficient interest to read and listen to the Dhamma is one way to create good karma – as long as the interest is skilful, for it is quite possible to produce bad karma while doing something that appears skilful. Complex as the subject may be, however, reminding ourselves of this principle of cause and effect can make it easier to let go of anger. So these are the five methods for eradicating any resentment we become aware of.

On a number of occasions, the Buddha recommended we keep away from situations that tend to stir us up. We should avoid encounters that give rise to anger, especially when our emotions are unstable and easily ignited – just as we should protect ourselves from bad people, wild elephants, jungle thickets, and other perils. While we should not run away from difficulties, it is perfectly acceptable to admit we cannot handle every situation with which we are confronted. We should try our best to manage circumstances with loving-kindness and compassion, but accept that sometimes we may be unable to cope.

Equanimity is regarded as the highest of emotions, and should not be confused with indifference. Not only does equanimity include loving-kindness – which indifference does not – but it arises from insight into impermanence, into the fact that things cannot be tomorrow as they are today. Within us and without, things change all the time; even our beliefs and views will be a little different by tomorrow, and any attempt to stand in the way of this process will usually involve suffering. Equanimity means accepting things as they are, so for someone endeavouring to make spiritual progress, it means not creating disharmony by interfering with other people's business.

Equanimity involves a sense of acceptance and peaceful contentment. So what can we do about suffering? Our first intention should
be to ensure we do nothing to increase it, then to approach each
situation with empathy and make any changes appropriately. If we
can make external changes without losing our inner peace, so much
the better, but in general we can make profound changes only to
ourselves, and that is difficult enough.

The next section of the sutta is a longer explication of the same
issue, by Sāriputta, the Buddha's 'right-hand man'. Sāriputta was
known for his wisdom, and often elaborated on the Buddha's discourses. When people asked the Buddha whether Sāriputta's teachings were correct, he invariably agreed.

> *Thus spoke the Venerable Sāriputta: 'There are five ways to*
> *overcome anger and resentment, through which we should be*
> *able to overcome anger and resentment. What are these five?*
> *If someone is not pure in deed but pure in word, anger and*
> *resentment against him should be overcome. If someone is*
> *not pure in word but pure in deed, anger and resentment*
> *against him should be overcome. Again, if someone is impure*
> *in deed and word but from time to time opens his heart to be*
> *filled with faith, anger and resentment against him should*
> *be overcome. Again, if someone is pure neither in deed nor in*
> *word, neither does his heart open from time to time to be*
> *filled with faith, anger and resentment against him should*
> *be overcome. Again, if someone is pure in deed and word,*
> *and time and again his heart opens to be filled with faith,*
> *anger and resentment against him should be overcome.'*

So Sāriputta lists five different types of people – and goes on to
illustrate, with little parables, how to get on with each of them,
restraining anger and resentment towards them. Our speech may be
virtuous but we behave badly, or what we say may be unskilful
though what we do is good. The third possibility is that both actions
and words may be blameworthy, but the heart is open. Fourthly,
even the heart is closed and hard. Lastly, words and deeds are
exemplary and the heart is open.

*How are we to overcome anger and resentment against the
first type of person? Like a monk clothed in rags who
beholds rags lying in the street, holds on to them with his
left foot, spreads them out with his right foot, cuts off
whatever there is of solid cloth, and takes it with him, so
with someone who is impure in deed but pure in word, one
should call to mind at that time not the impurity of his deed
but the purity of his word. In this way should anger and
resentment against him be overcome.*

In the Buddha's day all clothes were hand-woven and very expen-
sive, so monks and nuns used to wear patchwork robes. If they found
pieces of cloth on the road or among rubbish they could pick them
up and sew them together. In this parable, a monk sees some rags,
tears off what he can use, and leaves the rest behind. So this is how
to think of someone who acts unskilfully but whose speech is skilful:
we should disregard the bad deeds and consider only their words.
This is not to say we ignore the bad things they have done; we see
them but we don't pass judgement, because condemnation always
leads to resentment and anger. Very little is perfect in this world, so
theoretically we could be angry from first thing in the morning until
late at night. But if we focus on the virtues of someone with whom
we have become angry (presumably not without reason) we get the
chance to overcome our anger. They may have many bad points and
only a sprinkling of good, but we should still direct our attention to
the good.

It is we who derive the greatest benefit from doing so, because the
other person is probably unaware of our negativity. Even if we
express it, they are unlikely to be able to appreciate our feelings. It
might be useful to point out that something they have done is not
right, but it is utterly pointless to tell someone angrily that we feel
resentment towards them. The way to overcome our anger and
resentment and return to inner tranquillity is to consider their good
points. Inner turmoil just makes life more difficult than it is already.

Sāriputta now produces another illustration:

*Suppose the surface of a pond to be overgrown with slimy
weed and water plants, and that someone overcome by the
heat, sweating, worn out, thirsty, and thus in torment,*

approaches the pond, goes down to the pond, removes the
weed and plants at places with both hands, drinks with
cupped hands, and then goes on his way. In the same way
with a person of impure word but pure deed, one has to
contemplate not his impurity in speech but his purity in
action. Thus one should overcome anger and resentment
against such a person.

So we have this man walking along in the sweltering heat, exhausted
and thirsty. Because of the plants covering the surface of the water,
he is unable to quench his thirst immediately. But he uses his common sense and pushes away the weeds, drinks the water, and is
refreshed. Similarly, we can push aside the impure words of a person
and think of their good, pure actions. Let us remember, for example,
occasions when they have helped people, or consider their particular
qualities, and leave what is irritating about them out of the equation.

Such parables form a pithy and memorable aid to this practice. We
just imagine the rags lying there, worn and frayed, but reusable. Or
the weeds and water plants pushed aside to reveal pure, refreshing
water. Here is a third illustrative vignette:

Suppose a cow's footprint has a small amount of water in it,
and that someone overcome by the heat, sweating, worn out,
thirsty, and thus in torment, comes by and sees the water. He
thinks, 'If I scoop up the small quantity of water in this
cow's footprint with my hands or some container, I will
disturb it and make it undrinkable. Therefore I will rather go
down on all fours like a cow and sip the water, and then go
on my way.' And this is what he does. Likewise, with
someone who is impure in word and deed but whose heart
opens up from time to time and experiences faith, one should
not consider his impurity in word and deed at that time.
Instead, one should contemplate that his heart opens up
from time to time and attains faith. Thus one should
overcome anger and resentment against such a person.

If this person were to dip his hands or a container in the water it
would become muddy and undrinkable, and it is the same if we
think about what is worst in someone, what is ugly in their words

and actions: we get 'stirred up'. As this feeling becomes increasingly unpleasant we find no peace. It is significant that the person in the parable kneels down in order to drink, for we have to go down on our knees figuratively speaking and understand in all humility that we can find inner peace only when we learn to live with another person's unskilful words and deeds.

This parable is easy to remember, as drinking water from a footprint is not a nice thing to imagine. But if we are thirsty – representing the inner agitation that comes with anger and resentment – we will accept whatever drink we can find. We put up with what we find objectionable in someone, we avoid stirring it up, and consequently retain our inner peace. The person in the parable gets to drink something, and we too can find something to ease our relations with the person whose speech and action are so annoying. We remind ourselves that they have a heart that opens from time to time and has experienced faith. Moreover, even with regard to their words and deeds, we can recall that such a person has good in them too. Looking at them in this way we can make allowances and turn down the heat of our seething emotions.

Here is the fourth parable:

> *Imagine a sick man, seriously ill and suffering, walking along a road. He is a long way from any village, and cannot find food or medicine, or anyone to look after him or direct him. But then someone notices him and feels compassion, love, and goodwill with the thought, 'May that man find suitable food and medicine, someone to look after him and direct his course, lest he pass away!' Similarly, towards a person of impure deed and word, whose heart does not open to an experience of faith, we should feel compassion, love, and goodwill, with the thought, 'May this venerable one give up his bad practice in thought, word, and deed, and may he practise good thought, word, and deed; and may he not, when his body disintegrates after his death, end up in the lower worlds, on the path of suffering.' In this way should we overcome anger and resentment against such a person.*

This parable illustrates karmic connections, how someone will have to face the results of their own actions, and how we can therefore develop compassion for them. If we say or do or intend something unskilful, we are in truth suffering from hatred or greed, as though from an illness. Either we speak or act out of hatred, or our actions or words are rooted in greed. All human beings suffer in this way due to the poison of delusion that, as the Buddha explained, underlies the poisons of greed and hatred. They all cause discontent in us and turmoil in the world: in the family, in business, and between nations.

If greed and hatred can be regarded as illness, the Buddha can be seen as the great physician, and the Dhamma, his teaching, as medicine. This medicine may not always taste pleasant but it is guaranteed to cure us. The parable of the sick man who cannot find help is therefore particularly appropriate and memorable. We encounter so many people who are suffering because of their bad deeds, unskilful speech, and lack of faith, and the only reasonable response is one of compassion, with the hope that they will recover from their illness, find inner peace, and thus cease to reap the painful consequences. We wish everyone good physical health, so it should not be difficult to wish them another kind of good health as well: not to be laid low by greed and hatred. This way of looking at things can be very beneficial to our practice.

The fifth and final parable is more joyful:

Suppose there is a pond with clear water, refreshing water, cool water, sparkling water, in a beautiful location, an exquisite location, in the shade of green trees. And imagine that someone comes by overcome by the heat, sweating, worn out, thirsty, and thus in torment. He steps down into the pond, bathes, and drinks from the water. Then he climbs out again, and sits or lies down in the shade. Likewise, with someone of pure deed and word, whose heart opens up time and again and finds faith, we should at that time consider and contemplate his purity in word and deed, that his heart opens up time and again and finds faith. Thus one should overcome anger and resentment against such a person.

Someone who is pure in word and deed and whose heart opens up time and again is compared to a delightful pond, with clear water, cool and refreshing. Even if we feel hurt in some way by such a person, we can overcome any upsurge of resentment or anger by recognizing that they are a source of bliss for us and for others, and that there is nothing to which we can attach negative feelings, their conduct in life being so pure, and their emotional life so full of compassion and love. The discourse concludes with the following statement:

> *The mind can find peace in someone who in all possible ways gives rise to faith and confidence.*[*]

We can greatly fortify our inner peace by regular contact with some-one whom we completely trust. The Buddha often pointed out how important it is to keep good company and to have noble friends: people who lead a pure life, follow a spiritual path, and can help us do the same. Such a person will see the world differently from someone who is interested only in the mundane, and they can help us to do likewise. However, we need to maintain our trust in such a friend. If our faith in them is shaken, we will find no peace until we can re-establish it. Otherwise, it might be necessary to give up the friendship.

Anger and our craving to be loved are two sides of the same coin. In each case we have the same underlying difficulty. If someone hurts us, it may express their lack of love, but it could be because they didn't feel well or even that they just don't know how to deal with people. To us, however, their conduct comes across as rejection. If we want to be loved but are not shown any we will become sad and then angry. Love may well be the universal remedy that can make everyone emotionally and spiritually healthy – but this is not the love that requires an occasion and is dependent on finding someone lovable. After all, only an Enlightened One is entirely worthy of love. We direct our heart towards love, and when love has become a quality of our heart it no longer matters whether the object of our love returns our love or not. Whether the other person loves or cannot love makes no difference to us. The desire to be loved is only a function of the ego. If we are so unsure whether we are lovable or not that we prefer to leave the decision to others, we are certainly

---

[*] Aṅguttara-Nikāya v.162

lost anyway, because everyone regularly changes their opinion, as we change ours.

First we should establish in our own heart that we are indeed lovable, and with this in mind recognize that everyone else is equally lovable. Though we have the same faults as everyone, we are still worthy of love. Then we should recognize that we don't need to find someone else to love us, as the true source of love is found within. There will then be no need to be angry or even unhappy if someone doesn't care about us. Because they are not yet fully able to love, we can feel compassion for them.

So in giving up anger and resentment we have also to give up seeking love from others. Then the whole problem is resolved, because anger and resentment cannot possibly arise in a heart full of love. But feelings are fickle and our hearts unstable, and the overcoming of this instability is one of the most important aspects of spiritual practice. If we can win independence from the power of other people's emotions, and from external circumstances generally, by cultivating the inner power of love so that it no longer gives way to those forces, then we truly have a spiritual practice. Whether we ever come to the end of this practice is not the point; we just continue to follow the way of purification.

Thus have I heard. On a certain occasion the Exalted One,
while wandering through Kosala in the company of a great
number of monks, came to Kesaputta, a town of the
Kālāmas. Now the Kālāmas of Kesaputta heard it said that
Gotama, the ascetic, the Sakyā son, the Buddha who had
gone forth from palace to homelessness, had reached
Kesaputta. And this auspicious report concerning Gotama
the Exalted One was spread far and wide: 'It is he indeed
the Buddha, the Holy One, the Fully Enlightened One,
perfect in knowledge and practice, well-farer, knower of the
worlds, unsurpassed guide of those looking for guidance,
the Exalted One. He makes known this world together with
its good and bad spirits, with its host of ascetics and priests
and peoples, having come to know it and see through it for
himself. He teaches the teaching that is beautiful in the
beginning, beautiful in the middle, and beautiful in the end.
In letter and spirit he preaches the holy life that is utterly
pure. How excellent it is to see such a Holy One.'…

Aṅguttara-Nikāya iii.65

7

What Should We Believe?

THE KĀḶĀMA SUTTA is one of the most famous of the Buddha's discourses, and it is particularly relevant to people who want to follow a spiritual path but – faced with the huge number of teachings on offer – don't know which way to go. The Kāḷāmas were one of the many tribes in India at the time of the Buddha, who gave them guidelines to help them find the answer to this question.

The discourse starts with the words 'Thus have I heard', which identifies the text as one recited after the Buddha's death by Ānanda, the Buddha's cousin and his attendant for twenty years.

Thus have I heard. On a certain occasion the Exalted One, while wandering through Kosala in the company of a great number of monks, came to Kesaputta, a town of the Kāḷāmas. Now the Kāḷāmas of Kesaputta heard it said that Gotama, the ascetic, the Sakyā son, the Buddha who had gone forth from palace to homelessness, had reached Kesaputta. And this auspicious report concerning Gotama the Exalted One was spread far and wide: 'It is he indeed the Buddha, the Holy One, the Fully Enlightened One, perfect in knowledge and practice, well-farer, knower of the worlds, unsurpassed guide of those looking for guidance, the Exalted One. He makes known this world together with its good and bad spirits, with its host of ascetics and priests and peoples, having come to know it and see through it for himself. He teaches the teaching that is beautiful in the beginning,

*beautiful in the middle, and beautiful in the end. In letter
and spirit he preaches the holy life that is utterly pure. How
excellent it is to see such a Holy One.'*

*So the Kāḷāmas of Kesaputta went to the place where the
Buddha was staying. Some saluted him in reverence and sat
down to one side; others greeted the Exalted One and sat
down; others raised their hands to the Exalted One with
palms together; others proclaimed their name and family;
while others sat down without saying anything.*

It is clear from this passage that the Kāḷāmas are not disciples of the
Buddha. They know it's very important to go and visit the Buddha,
but they are not all agreed on whether it is also important to hear
him. They simply have an interest in spiritual teachings, and the
Buddha's reputation – which has travelled ahead of him – is that he
is very good at explaining the teaching of self-purification. Everyone
greets the Buddha in the way they feel is appropriate. One can
imagine that the occasion might have been a bit of a shambles, with
hundreds of people arriving, bowing, offering greetings, announc-
ing their names, or just trying to find a place to sit. Had they all been
his disciples things would have been much quieter: everyone would
have just bowed and sat down – but that is clearly not the case here.
Here the audience are people on a spiritual quest who have heard
good things about Siddhattha Gotama of the Sakyā clan, or the
Buddha as he had become.

*As they were sitting thus, the Kāḷāmas of Kesaputta
addressed the Exalted One.*

Perhaps the chief elder of the town got to his feet and announced
the problem that it seems they shared:

*'Certain ascetics and brahmins come to Kesaputta. As to
their own view they proclaim and expound it in full, but the
views of others they abuse and revile, disparage and
undermine. Then again, different ascetics and brahmins* [the
priestly caste – not every brahmin is a priest, but every priest
is a brahmin] *on coming to Kesaputta do likewise: they*

proclaim and expound in full only their own view; the views of others they abuse and revile, disparage and undermine. Therefore we are in doubt, we are bewildered as to which of these ascetics and brahmins speaks the truth and which speaks falsehood.'

This of course is what makes the discourse so famous: every intelligent person nowadays knows this feeling. From each and every side we hear something different, and so many of those who present us with their beliefs and views manage to sound almost equally convincing. So here, the Kāḷāmas also observe that speakers trumpet their ideas at the expense of others, disparage the views of others, and declare their own beliefs to be the only valid ones. As a result, the Kāḷāmas have become very confused and doubtful about what to believe. This is the Buddha's answer:

'Yes, Kāḷāmas, you may well doubt, you may well waver. In a matter about which one cannot be sure doubt has arisen within you.'

The Buddha agrees; he understands how they may well be doubtful in the face of so many different views, especially since the various priests have also abused and reviled each other. He therefore supplies them with ten guidelines, which are now well known. Needless to say, these guidelines are intended for us too, and it is interesting that the Buddha advises that he himself, and his own teaching, should be judged by these guidelines. He subsequently offers the corresponding guidelines by which one may find one's true bearings, but to start with he lists criteria that are to be regarded as invalid or insufficient.

'Be not misled by hearsay,... or by what other people tell you,... or by tradition,...'

So do not believe something just because it has been handed down from generation to generation, from teacher to student, and is therefore called tradition. An emphasis on the authenticity of a tradition proves nothing.

'… or by fashionable views,…'

Don't be misled by the fact that a belief is conventional, well known, or modishly popular. That does not necessarily make it wrong, but it should not be the sole reason for going along with the trend.

'… or by the authority of sacred scriptures,…'

We should not rely solely on the authority of sacred scriptures. The discourses of the Buddha are not regarded as sacred anyway. It may well be appropriate to take a venerable Buddhist text very seriously, but the idea of automatically assigning authority to sacred texts is strongly rejected.

'… or by mere reasoning or logical inference,…'

Neither reason nor logic is sufficient to guarantee the truth or spiritual efficacy of a teaching.

'… or by theoretical speculation or personal opinion,…'

This stricture is directed against the whole range of cherished views and opinions, the customary modes of thought in which we get stuck by force of habit. And there are so many ways we hold opinions: in thoughts and through exercising our imagination, by subjective approval and acceptance, and by personal choice or preference. So we should not give way to the ever-present temptation to allow ourselves to be guided by our favoured notions and opinions.

'… or by the impression of personal merits and character of a particular teacher, or by the authority of a master.…'

Not even these are good enough reasons to follow a particular spiritual path. Uniquely in the history of religion, the Buddha does not tell people to accept someone's authority, whether natural, divine, assumed, or appointed, as a spiritual teacher, and that includes even his own. He himself had many positive qualities and was allegedly very charismatic and utterly confident and convincing – in other words, he was an authority – but even his own authority is, according to him, unacceptable as the sole reason for accepting his teachings.

> 'When you, Kālāmas, know for yourselves: "these things are unskilful, these things are reprehensible, these things are censured by the wise and when performed and undertaken lead to misfortune and sorrow," then, indeed, you may renounce them.'

The Buddha makes it clear that everyone is responsible for themselves, that everyone has to examine and know, not just offer blind faith and obsequious obedience. If one doesn't know what is reprehensible and blameworthy, one has to carry on searching.

The Buddha then asks:

> 'What do you think, Kālāmas: when greed arises in someone, is it to their benefit or misfortune?'
> 'To their misfortune, Sir.'
> 'In greed, Kālāmas, overcome by greed, losing control of the mind through craving, one takes life, takes what is not given, violates someone's spouse, speaks falsely, and encourages others to do the same; and this will lead to one's detriment and suffering for a long time.'
> 'That is indeed the case, Sir.'
> 'What do you think, Kālāmas: when hatred and delusion arise in someone, is it to their benefit or misfortune?'
> 'To their misfortune, Sir.'
> 'In hatred and delusion, Kālāmas, overcome by hatred and illusion, losing control of the mind through hatred and delusion, one takes life, takes what is not given, violates someone's spouse, speaks falsely, and encourages others to do the same; this will be to their loss and suffering for a long time.'
> 'That is indeed the case, Sir.'

So if craving arises – and murder, theft, adultery, and dishonesty all spring from craving – then we offend against the first four precepts. Hatred, likewise, can lead to the same misdeeds. The Buddha explains here that this moral code is the basis for the spiritual path. If we want to be 'spiritual' yet at the same time break these ethical precepts, we have little chance of turning that 'spirituality' into true spiritual development.

> *'What do you think, Kāḷāmas: are these things unskilful or*
> *skilful?'*
> *'Unskilful, Sir.'*
> *'Are they blameworthy or blameless?'*
> *'Blameworthy, Sir.'*
> *'Are these things praised or censured by the wise?'*
> *'Censured, Sir.'*
> *'And do these things conduce to loss and suffering, or not?*
> *How is it with them?'*
> *'These things do indeed conduce to loss and suffering. That is*
> *how we see it.'*

So the Buddha asks his audience what they themselves believe, and leaves them to come to their own conclusions.

> *'For this very reason, then, do we say thus: Do not be misled*
> *by hearsay, or by tradition, or by fashionable views, or by*
> *the authority of sacred scriptures, or by mere reasoning or*
> *logical inference, or by theoretical speculation or preferred*
> *opinions, or by someone's apparent advantage of person or*
> *character, or even by the authority of a master. Only when*
> *you know for yourselves: "These things are unwholesome,*
> *they are reprehensible, they are censured by the wise, and*
> *when performed and undertaken they conduce to loss and*
> *sorrow," then, indeed, you may renounce them.'*

The teacher shows the way, but we are not simply to follow the authority of a master, and we should not believe that a master can lead us to the goal without our involvement. None of the ideas we cherish can help us unless we clearly recognize what is skilful and what is not.

> *'But if you recognize for yourselves: "These things are*
> *wholesome, they are irreproachable, they are praised by the*
> *wise, and when undertaken and performed they are*

conducive to happiness and well-being," then you should adopt them.'

Then the Buddha talks about the opposite of craving: freedom from craving:

> *'What do you think, Kāḷāmas: freedom from craving, when it arises in someone, is it conducive to their benefit or misfortune?'*
> *'To their benefit, Sir.'*
> *'Free from craving, not overcome by craving, one's mind not out of control through craving, one abstains from taking life, abstains from taking the not given, abstains from sexual misconduct, abstains from untruthful speech, neither does one encourage others in these kinds of wrongdoing. Such will be conducive to one's happiness and well-being for a long time.'*
> *'Indeed that is so, Sir.'*
> *'What do you believe, Kāḷāmas, freedom from hatred and freedom from illusion, when they arise in someone, are they conducive to their benefit or misfortune?'*
> *'To their benefit, Sir.'*
> *'Free from hatred and illusion, not overcome by hatred and illusion, with one's mind not out of control, one does not kill, one does not steal, one does not covet the sexual partner of another, one does not lie, neither does one encourage others to do these things; and such will be conducive to one's happiness and well-being for a long time.'*
> *'Indeed that is so, Sir.'*
> *What do you think, Kāḷāmas, are these things skilful or unskilful?'*
> *'Skilful, Sir.'*
> *'Blameworthy or blameless?'*
> *'Irreproachable, Sir.'*
> *'Are these things censured or praised by the wise?'*
> *'Praised, Sir.'*
> *'And these things, if undertaken and practised, are they conducive to well being or not? How is it with them?'*

*'These things if undertaken and practised lead to happiness
and well-being. That is how we see it.'*

The Buddha very often advises us to question our conscience in
order to distinguish between the skilful and the unskilful. If this
investigation is inconclusive, we should discuss it with someone
trustworthy and wise, but in the end we each need to arrive at our
own conclusion in order to develop insight. Nobody can do the work
for us.

So this is the list of ten things that should not be allowed to mislead
us. Firstly, hearsay: we should not believe what we are told without
thinking about it independently. We should not be influenced by
friends or family to such an extent that we unthinkingly adopt their
opinions because we don't want to be thought different.

Secondly, we should not allow ourselves to be misled by blind
adherence to tradition. Old customs are assumed to be right simply
because they have been followed for so long, but they cannot be
valid, because they represent paths that have led to loss and misfortune.

Thirdly, fashionable views. The influence of modern media-driven
intellectual fashions can often be harmful, because they usually go
unnoticed. They start in childhood and eventually set themselves up
as our own opinions. We have been led to believe in something we
have not thought through – just accepted as the most persuasive
opinion on offer. As the text makes clear, this is not just a modern
phenomenon. It has always been the case.

Fourthly, the authority of sacred writings. This has of course been
the cause of a great deal of trouble, because all scriptures, even
so-called sacred ones, have actually been written down by human
beings, and human beings can get things wrong. Anything written
is subject to error; it has all the limitations of human weakness.

As for the next two, concerning insufficient foundation for belief,
there is no doubt that giving priority to the intellect and logical
inference has its advantages. Nevertheless, reason alone also has its
dangers, as it can tend towards limited and materialistic goals and
ignore the spiritual dimension. If we fail to unite head and heart and
just think logically, we may indeed be using our intellectual faculties
appropriately, but we are in constant danger of employing them to
the wrong ends and going in the wrong direction. But the mind is a
magician and can turn in any direction; as soon as the heart takes

part in our thought, introducing emotion and the capacity to love, we are on an entirely different level of understanding.

Then come favoured personal ideas and speculative theories. These were as popular then as they are today. We naturally tend to believe our own theories – that certainly hasn't changed in 2,500 years – but they can have serious consequences if they are not valid, and it is not easy to determine the validity of a theory: one person might think it brilliant, another might call it deceptive, while another won't know either way. We must investigate and experiment to see for ourselves whether something is skilful or unskilful.

Finally, what is being taught? Is it as good as it claims to be, or could it mislead us? It is easy to be dazzled by charismatic teachers, but an attractive appearance is no guarantee that the teaching is going to be true or appropriate. Even today, spiritual masters are able to exert a significant level of influence by their mere presence. Although propaganda is communicated to the public at large in a variety of new formats, it still travels from person to person much as before.

After running through this list, the Buddha continues:

> 'However, if you recognize for yourselves: "These things are skilful, irreproachable, praised by the wise, and are, if undertaken and performed, conducive to bliss and well being," then, Kālāmas, you may confidently adopt them.... Such is the reason for my words to you just now. In such a way, freed from craving and ill will, with an unconfused mind, clear in understanding and suffused with awareness, the noble disciple radiates loving-kindness, compassion, sympathetic joy, and equanimity to all the quarters of the world.'

If we are freed from craving and ill will, from greed and hatred, the mind is no longer confused and can be objective and discriminating in its judgements. A mind deeply stained by covetousness and anger is clouded. Craving and aversion are deeply subjective reactions, and if they are relinquished, the mind becomes objective. No longer confused, it is clear, radiant in knowledge, and aware. If we are mindful we cannot at the same time cultivate unkindness or desire. Therefore the Buddha again and again advocates mindfulness, so that we learn to see ourselves and the world objectively and realistically. This eradicates our subjective colouring of events. Instead of 'I want this' and 'I prefer not to have to put up with that,' we see things as they really are.

Mindfulness helps us to cultivate the four highest emotions: loving-kindness, compassion, sympathetic joy, and equanimity – tradition-ally called the four sublime abodes, or divine abidings, because entry into these states of mind is literally 'heavenly'; it is like going to paradise. At stages in the course of our practice we may focus on one or other in particular, though we can move through all four of them in succession in the course of just a few minutes. Equanimity can be developed gradually through insight. If we are less caught up in wanting and not wanting, we will see more clearly that everything changes all the time, so it is not worth getting upset about anything. And of course this recognition paves the way for equanimity.

Equanimity may appear similar to apathy or indifference, so it must be carefully distinguished from these negative emotions. Indif-ference is called the near enemy of equanimity, because although it appears similar it has very different consequences; it effectively becomes armour plating, because we allow nothing to come close to us. This may make us feel slightly more safe, but it expresses and reinforces our insecurity. The lack of love and compassion in the feeling of indifference leaves us exposed and vulnerable on the sidelines of life: a spectator instead of a participant. Indifference appears to be a good way to protect ourselves, but in fact the best protection is our own loving-kindness. As long as we are carrying love and compassion in our hearts we are completely safe from having to entertain such unpleasant feelings as hatred, ill will, jeal-ousy, envy, pride, revulsion, or aversion. Thus purified, our inner life will consequently be peaceful and at ease.

> *'With such a mind, a mind free from hatred and ill will, and free from anxiety and defilements, the noble disciple is certain, in this very lifetime, of a fourfold consolation.'*

The Buddha mentions this consolation to the Kālāmas only because while they are intelligent people they are not yet his followers, and it is up to them to decide what they want to do. Many of us nowadays are in the same plight – in search of something that can lift us from our inner darkness and liberate us from anxiety. But the Buddha never categorically said 'Follow me!' He simply outlined the truth, and the path of practice to its realization. If his advice appeals, one should follow it; if it doesn't, one should carry on as before. The Buddha did not offer encouragement to the proselytizing tendency; he only expounded his teaching to those who wanted to listen. According to that teaching, when the mind no longer needs to cling to anything or be angry with anyone, an inner joy arises, and it is light and free from anxiety. Conversely, our flimsy justifications for heartless behaviour fall apart as the mind is no longer burdened with these anxieties and becomes purified. The fourfold consolation the Buddha offers the Kālāmas is as follows:

'If there is a world beyond, and if there is fruit, a ripening of deeds good and bad, then when the body disintegrates after death one may be reborn among joyful beings, in a heavenly world. One is certain of this consolation.'

That is to say, if we believe that actions have consequences and that there is an afterworld, then we can – if we have performed good deeds – expect a pleasant time after death. This first consolation is a certainty.

'If on the other hand there is no world beyond, and no fruit, no ripening of deeds good and bad, then one lives a happy life in this world, without suffering, free from hatred and ill will. One may be certain, too, of this second consolation.'

So the Buddha is saying that even if we do not believe in rebirth and that actions have ongoing consequences in this way, then at least we can enjoy life here and now, being free, due to our state of purification, from ill will, anxiety, and affliction. We can be sure of this second consolation.

'Now if harm befalls one who has done harm, and yet we have no harmful intentions, how can sorrow touch us who do no harm? One may be certain of this third consolation.'

So we now take the case of there being no afterlife, but results of our actions in this world. On this basis, if we do nothing bad we can at least be sure we will not suffer negative results in this life. We can be sure of this third consolation.

> 'But if no evil befalls one who has done harm, then we know ourselves to be pure in this life on both these counts. One may be certain of this fourth consolation.'

Finally, then, if we do not believe our actions have consequences, if we do not believe the karmic law of cause and effect, we will still have the security of a good conscience. We may be sure of this fourth consolation.

> 'With such a mind, a mind free from hatred and ill will, free from anxiety and undefiled, the noble disciple is certain of this fourfold consolation in this very life.'

We can enjoy this fourfold consolation here and now. We do not have to wait for future events to confirm that we have not been wasting our time. If we have done no ill, we need fear no ill. If we have done good, we can be sure that good will come of it. If there are no hidden results of our actions, at least we need have no fear of ill befalling us.

Apparently the Kālāmas were delighted to hear this, and they reply:

> 'So it is, O Exalted One! With such a mind free from hatred, free from ill will, free from anxiety and defilement, the noble disciple is certain of this fourfold consolation even in this very life. Excellent, excellent! It is as if that which was overturned were set up again, or that which was hidden were discovered, or as if the one who was lost had been shown the way, or as if light had been brought into darkness, so that all who had eyes might see things clearly. In such fashion the Exalted One has demonstrated the teaching in manifold ways. We go for refuge to the Exalted One, and to the teaching, and to the community of monks! May the Exalted One receive us as his followers, as such who have gone for refuge from today for the rest of their lives.'

They are all sufficiently convinced by the Buddha for them to feel able to commit themselves to him as their teacher, to the Dhamma, his teaching, and to the Sangha, the community of those who practise his teaching, and by doing this they become his students.

The spiritual open-mindedness displayed here is quite unique for that time: everyone is understood as having to make up their own mind with regard to the spiritual path. Only one's conscience, or the advice of wise and sensible people, or one's own observation of what appear to be the results of one's actions, are recommended as reference points. The Buddha's message seems to be that we should beware of falling prey to the influence of plausible belief systems – which can take place in very subtle ways, especially under charismatic teachers or those who are seen as spiritual authorities. And we should never lose sight of this message – not in order to foster sceptical doubt regarding the teacher or the teaching, but in order to investigate the teaching for what is true within ourselves.

We are our own best teachers, inasmuch as what we need to know is, in the end, to be found within us; and with some application in terms of self-observation we can get to know ourselves in this way more and more deeply. On what are my spiritual ambitions based? Of what does my spiritual path consist? What should I do in order to purify myself? Am I talking myself into believing something or do I wholeheartedly practise it? The point of this discourse is to enable us to realize that what we need to do is not merely to believe something, but to investigate and know ourselves.

We lead a spiritual life in order to overcome and burst through seven fetters. What are these seven? The fetter of attraction, the fetter of aversion, the fetter of views, the fetter of doubt, the fetter of conceit, the fetter of envy, and the fetter of self-addiction. If in someone these seven fetters are overcome, utterly destroyed, uprooted like a palm tree from its soil, entirely annihilated and unable to rise again, then it may be said that this person has cut off craving, cast off the fetters, and through complete insight into the nature of conceit has made an end to all suffering.

Aṅguttara-Nikāya vii.8–9

8

The Seven Fetters

IN THIS DISCOURSE the Buddha deals – somewhat succinctly – with the seven fetters that hold us back from happiness and freedom. The passage is reproduced opposite in its entirety. In a brief and conclusive address we are informed that we have only to destroy seven fetters in order to be free from all suffering. But these fetters are attachments, which keep us imprisoned, and we are all, internally, held within their grip. Working on them, therefore, takes a lot of will-power.

Attraction
The first does not sound much like a fetter. In fact it sounds like something quite agreeable. Of course it is good to be attracted to people, but only as long as this does not involve misunderstanding the nature of love as clinging and attachment, because this is where all our difficulties lie – this is what we are constantly up against when we love people and fail to understand love as a faculty of the heart. Instead, what we call love is the way attraction immediately solidifies into attachment and the desire to possess, and dependence upon the object of our desire returning our attentions. We cannot manage without their presence, care, and fidelity.

This type of love is always tainted with fear and clouded by hatred. Fear and hatred have the same negative qualities: inasmuch as it is impossible to fear what we truly love, it is only what we fear that can engender hatred in us. We fear losing the one we love. This is not to say that we hate them: what we hate is the thought of losing them and their love.

Once we have picked one or two people (from the six billion people on earth) to love, they are supposed to love us, too. If that doesn't happen, or if we lose them, whether through death, or because they change their views or the object of their love, we experience it as a tragedy. But this is not an accurate interpretation of the meaning of love or life, and not in accord with the Buddha's teaching.

The point of living and loving is to develop more fully our heart's capacity to love. Just as the intellect is trained by our efforts to understand information, the heart needs opportunities to evolve, too, and any effort at love allows the heart to mature. The heart's only purpose is to love, and if we exercise it only with certain selected people and situations, we narrow down the heart's capacity to grow, and build walls around us that then imprison us.

When attraction is combined with attachment, one's evolution as an individual is severely hampered. Attachment means clinging to people – or often just one person – and this blocks the development of our capacity to love, which must be unconditional in order to evolve freely. When it is unconditional we no longer choose certain people to love, whether those we find attractive, or those who are prepared to love us, or those who have shown their love for us first.

All these conditions that we put upon our love limit it. But, limited as it is, such conditional love is responsible for daily tragedy, fear, and ceaseless inner turmoil, and it can never liberate the heart. The teaching of the Buddha is the teaching of liberation from all suffering. That our daily life becomes more pleasant through this practice is a side-effect, not the main point of the teaching. In order to understand its meaning, we need to completely reverse our normal way of thinking, and part and parcel of this reorientation is the cultivation of the heart's capacity to love. This cannot happen just like that, but we can look at all our encounters with others as opportunities to learn, and start working within those situations.

The perfect opportunity occurs when we come up against those we find least attractive, because we can develop love within such a relationship that is going to be less dependent on conditions, and everything else we need to do to cultivate love will naturally flow from that. This may be difficult to start with, and we may find it less of a strain to begin by training ourselves to care more for people towards whom we tend to feel rather neutral. Of course, we have no problems loving those we find attractive, but to learn to love those in whom we are not normally interested is an exercise in the right direction. Ultimately, we will even have to love those we don't find lovable. If we don't make that effort, we hurt ourselves at the deepest level, and our heart will always be uneasy.

Aversion

The second fetter, aversion, arises from our inability to feel un-bounded love. Most people don't expect to live a life free from aversion, and find it too much trouble to try to overcome it – after all, we are born with aversions already in place, otherwise we would not have come into this world. However, aversion encompasses hatred, ill will, and anger, and these emotions have very negative effects. Although attraction is ultimately just as harmful, antagonis-tic emotions have a stronger deleterious effect on us.

Most people only try to get rid of their aversion once it has escalated into hatred and anger, and this is often done in a com-pletely inappropriate way, by avoiding the people who seem to provoke our aversion. This is an impossible endeavour, as we will never be able to steer clear of unpleasant experiences, and that includes the company of unpleasant people. Avoiding them is not a solution; running away from the problem is not going to solve it. There are situations in which we are forced to retreat because the circumstances are just too much for us. When this happens, we have to admit to ourselves that we are unable to feel love in every situ-ation, rather than use the excuse that the other person is insufferable. This is a failure that shows up ourselves, and no one else.

Everything takes place in our own heart. We do not need a special place for the spiritual life, no specific clothes, no esoteric language; it is enough to know that everything is down to us, and that experi-ences and feelings, other people, and external circumstances, have no function other than to act as triggers. Only when we see this will we be able to embark on the spiritual life, and as long as we think that the world around us is to blame, we cannot practise it. Expecting others to change for the better is essentially self-defeating, because in the end everyone does what they consider to be right by their own standards, not by ours.

Any one of us can find ourselves unable to cope with a situation and try to get out of it, but if we are following a spiritual path we should only take refuge in flight after we have made a number of unsuccessful attempts to love the person or persons involved. We will then understand that our irritation, hatred, and aversion are training grounds, and the other people involved are our teachers. They help us to find out what is going on inside ourselves.

We lose any trace of freedom as soon as we become stuck in our own emotions – whether attraction or aversion. We cannot be free if we are entangled by attraction or driven by aversion – and in the end the two types of reactions go together, as they are both variations on the theme of attachment. The more personal preferences we have, the more personal aversions there are within us. Conversely, the more free from attachment we are, the more we can develop a feeling of warmth and solidarity with others.

The positive counterpart of aversion is loving-kindness, and the Buddha has strongly recommended cultivating this towards all beings through the *mettā bhāvanā* (loving-kindness) meditation. Above all, his advice is to use every confrontation with another person as a training opportunity. Every day, from morning to night, we have a chance to regard others as teachers, wherever we encounter them, and to meet them with love; we always have the opportunity to act with a loving heart, and without attachment.

Our love gets blocked by prejudice, critical appraisal, comparison, and judgement even though it is certainly not the point of human life to assume the role of judge, whether over oneself or over others. But the fact is that we often judge others and we should therefore make it clear to ourselves that this is a waste of time and energy, and hinders the development of a loving heart.

It is interesting that the Buddha likened ill will to a dysfunction of the gall bladder for, even today, when someone is irritable we call them bilious. The point he is making is that it is not the object of our anger who is afflicted and ill-tempered, but ourselves.

The Buddha also likened ill will and aversion to a wind blowing over the surface of a pond, whipping up waves that make it impossible to see our reflection. In the same way, anger and aversion preclude self-knowledge, because the emotional agitation denies us a clear view of ourselves. This is the cause of much unhappiness in human relationships, of friendships falling apart and growing inner disquiet. Unsure how we should respond to others, we avoid everyone except those on whose goodwill and friendliness we can rely – though even here we have no guarantee of a friendly reception. The problem is over-attachment to the emotional support of others; we seek praise and run away from blame – which is such a waste of energy. As long as we continue to be prisoners of our feelings and problems, our relationships with others will perhaps work superficially, but not on a deep, heart-to-heart level. We will have sufficient confidence in our own responses, and not to have to wait for others to be friendly and approving before we are prepared to go out to them – only when we have learned to cultivate the heart – to develop our capacity to love. We have to learn to view everything as a chance to sort ourselves out; and with a clearer view and understanding of ourselves we will be more in harmony with others.

We can make use of any situation in this way. Everyone we meet can help us to see ourselves better – whether it is a postman, neighbour, colleague, or just someone in the car beside ours, or someone who takes our parking place. We are always free to generate a loving heart. This will be much easier if we recognize that everyone is in the same situation; if we can recognize that although our suffering comes from ourselves alone, we have no monopoly on it. Suffering is universal, and all the individual cases we come across are variations on the same theme. Human existence is imbued with suffering at every moment, every day, every hour. Naturally, we should like to sidestep it, but that is just not possible. Once we accept this, life becomes much simpler, and as compassion for the suffering all around us arises, we will have fewer problems in our relationships with others.

Views

The third fetter is made up of all those opinions and personal views that form the basis of the way we feel able to keep passing judgement. Ultimately, these are all wrong, according to the Buddha, because they are based on the dualistic perspective by which we refer to 'me' and 'you'. This perspective allows us to imagine that our ideas about what is good and what is bad actually represent the truth. We live in a relative world in which there are different ways to see things. As a result, we will find the views of others differ from our own. What we see as good or beautiful is bad or ugly for someone else.

Short of Enlightenment, we have no access to absolute truth – and it will be impossible even then to make a judgement on anything with which everyone agrees, because unenlightened beings can appreciate only relative truth.

This means the world we inhabit is a fantasy world, because there is a difference between our views and desires on the one hand and reality on the other. Things are never the way we would like them to be, of course, and we react with aversion to aspects of our experience that do not correspond to this fantasy. In this world, therefore, there can only be wrong views, but we continue to make use of these personal views as the moral foundation of the way we live our whole life – of all our desires and actions.

On the level of absolute truth we are no longer taking a view of the truth; we can only experience it. And when we experience absolute truth there is no longer any need to judge or condemn, no need to grasp at anything or recoil from it. When we experience everything as constantly subject to change, as coming into being and ceasing to be in continuous alternation, from millisecond to millisecond, there is no need to get upset about anything. If we are to educate our minds and hearts in such a way that love and understanding can grow, the main obstacle we have to deal with consists of our opinions. We are so full of them that we are unable to learn anything afresh.

The Buddha likens this condition of our mind to a clay vessel filled to the brim with water so that no more can be poured in. When we encounter new things we naturally check whether or not they fit with our established opinions before we accept them. But on that basis the way remains blocked, because a true spiritual path, being based in absolute truth, can never accord with those personal opinions. So the more opinions we have, the more difficult is the spiritual life. Conversely, a child-like openness can help us, the ability to see new things just as they are without prejudice. As adults, we habitually insist on the reliability of our recollections or the irrefutability of our ideas on how things should be. But one of the greatest moments of insight occurs when we see things as they really are and not as we had previously imagined them. Being unsubstantiated by absolute objectivity, our subjective notions are never likely to reflect reality, yet we climb aboard any passing bandwagon of fashionable opinion, rendering ourselves dependent on the opinions of others instead of being self-reliant and thinking things through for ourselves.

The Buddha said of himself that he is no more than a guide, and it is for us to make use of the methods he demonstrated in investigating the reality of life for ourselves. Whatever we turn to – human beings, ourselves, life, the world – what we seek are pleasant feelings and emotions, with the hope that unpleasant ones vanish as quickly as possible. This is absurd, of course: what is pleasant does not last and what is unpleasant cannot be kept at bay for very long.

Simply having a body is enough to make life unpleasant. It requires our constant attention, and having set ourselves the impossible task of maintaining a state of uninterrupted well-being, we can develop a preoccupation with staying healthy that can actually get us quite stressed. Exerting ourselves in the pursuit of anything apart from the spiritual goal – and that includes the quest for what is pleasant – is inimical to the spiritual life. The spiritual life is a quest not for what is pleasant, but for what is true, for insight into the nature of things as they really are.

The first thing we observe in things as they really are is that they change from one moment to the next. Each day is over all too soon, and our life passes swiftly. All the thoughts that have ever passed through our mind have vanished. We might write a few down with meticulous care and detail, but we will never recapture the thoughts as they were in their freshness. Feelings and sensations we remember are simply no longer there, yet we still believe we are something solid. When we look at old photos of ourselves we might say, 'Yes, I remember that,' but memories are totally unreliable – they are interpretations of our past. If we look at photos of ourselves honestly, the idea of our solidity becomes absurd.

In this way, and in the general course of our spiritual practice, we can gradually acknowledge that every moment is transitory, and start to understand what it is that absolute truth might be. Normally, everything we experience is relative, and this kind of reality is what we are trying to contact through the senses, when we see, hear, taste, smell, touch, and think. It can never be a completely successful exercise in terms of experiencing what is really going on, because its aim is to make us cosy and comfortable. With this aim in view the mind immediately categorizes sense contacts as either pleasant or unpleasant, and no true perception arises because everyone thinks and feels slightly differently about things. One view of things can never be true for everyone: the sound of cowbells and the smell of manure might have pleasant associations for some, while others might find them unpleasant and distracting. So everything we experience via the nose, eyes, ears, mouth, and by touch, is completely individual and immediately linked to a personal view. These views make our life difficult and condition our aversions and attractions. We are forever pulled between the two, back and forth, up and down, like a seesaw.

In order to bring this unsatisfactory state to an end and find peace, our hearts and minds have to work together to create understood experience. We must experience events as they really are, not how we imagine them. The Buddha likened the way we lead our lives to children playing in a house that catches fire. We refuse to leave because we do not want to leave our toys – the views that keep us in the house. So 'wrong views' are not so much about failing to grasp what's going on in our daily life and arriving at mistaken conclusions. Rather, they represent our tendency to form opinions, assessments, and judgements about things. The inquiry into the way things really are, on the other hand, takes practice, it takes time, and it takes the will to realize the truth. With such a will it is possible for anyone to achieve true insight.

Doubt

The next fetter, doubt as a fixed state of mind, is sometimes called sceptical doubt. The Buddha likened it to lost travellers, going round in circles in the desert, with no map or provisions. Eventually they are robbed and killed by bandits. Doubt as a fetter is the tendency to refer everything to our own opinions, and to discard whatever does not fit with them. If our convictions are strong enough, we will doubt anything that does not accord with our own opinions.

In order to be able to see a fresh viewpoint, we have to be prepared to doubt our own views. Meditation is a good way to begin this process: anyone who has meditated at least a few times should know that our thoughts are essentially untrustworthy. They arise without being invited, and the next moment are gone. Moreover, they are often nonsensical. If we get up from our meditation and carry on taking these thoughts seriously, without questioning the opinions on which they are based, we haven't been paying attention in our meditation.

It takes a while before we reach a point in our meditation when we can be so concentrated that thoughts no longer arise. In the meantime, the meditator has the opportunity to experience thoughts as movements of the mind, just as the breath is a movement of the body, to see that both phenomena just come and go. It should then become clear that thoughts certainly don't equal truth. When we start calling into question all our views and judgements, we will start to become free from sceptical doubt as a fetter, and be able to start dropping our views and opening up to new possibilities. Doubt will then no longer be a fetter but an openness to something new.

This is quite a challenge, because our thinking has followed familiar tracks and patterns all our life, and an attitude of sceptical doubt with respect to what goes in the opposite direction is endemic in us, making the spiritual path all the more difficult. It requires a complete reversal of direction – not in the sense of no longer being able to live in the world, but as a complete change in our attitudes.

Doubt as a fetter is also an issue in most people's everyday relationships. Not having developed the heart's capacity to love, we not only doubt our own abilities: we allow ourselves to accept other people's doubts about us. Such an attitude is totally unnecessary: if others don't accept us, that is their attitude and their karma. This is the first thing we need to realize – that whatever others do is their concern, not ours, and we do not need to react to it. We are quick to take on other people's reactions to us as something to do with us, when really they are daily occurrences that happen to be taking place around us. We don't get worked up about what someone in Africa might be doing or saying at this moment; why, then, do we get so bothered by what our neighbour has just done or said – which in reality is no more important to us? The important thing in our relations with others is the need for us to cultivate love.

Whilst doubt holds sway we can never be sure whether something is helpful or good for us, whether we will be able to do something, whether others will favour or endorse something. In order to be able to follow the teaching of the Buddha we have first of all to stop thinking in that way. Only by trying it out can we find out whether it is good and skilful and what kind of effect it will have.

Conceit

The fetter of conceit consists less in conceited, arrogant behaviour than in being convinced, intellectually and emotionally, that we have something about us that is fixed and separate and that needs protection. This is the greatest fetter of all. Ego-conceit, the belief that we are someone – and what's more, someone special, someone clever – is the fundamental form of conceit, creating constant trouble for us, which will continue to make life a strain as long as we hold to it. It is as an ego that we are under the illusion that we know what's what, and run after things that are pleasant, avoiding what is unpleasant. The ego is an illusion, a fantasy in which the whole of mankind dwells, and which causes immense damage. The single reason for which human beings wage war, cheat, murder, and steal is that they want to be safe and protect their ego.

We believe in the ego in the same way we as we believe in any imagined idea. Ego-conceit has implanted itself in the seedbed of our thinking processes, and as a consequence it has developed roots deep within our emotional territory: if we think something long enough we will also feel it. As long as we see ourselves as a separate person and keep thinking in this way, we will keep bringing up 'I, me, myself' as a continuous source of problems and worry. We will continue to take this drama, and the backdrop against which we perform, absolutely seriously. When we sit down in front of the television and watch a movie we don't take it as real – but we take our life very seriously indeed, even though it is made up of essentially the same stuff.

Ego-conceit is a fundamental difficulty upon which all other difficulties hang, and we cannot hope to resolve it immediately – the fetters of aversion, attraction, and doubt have to be worked on first. Following the path of practice that consists of the spiritual guidelines of the Buddha doesn't lead to the destruction of our self, but allows us to drop and see through the ego-illusion, so that one day we will find that all our fuss and exertion has been for nothing, and our life will seem like a movie played out before our eyes.

Envy

The fetter of envy is a form of hatred and a failure of love. It arises from a failure to understand that we belong to a totality from which the impulse to separate can only be harmful. By the same token, it

can be counteracted by sympathetic joy, which arises from the realization that we all belong together and that it makes no difference to
whom something good happens. We are all here on this earth
together, at the same time. We are all made of the same components.
Whether we are aware of it or not, we are all interconnected. If bad
things happen somewhere, we are all affected. When a war breaks
out on the other side of the world, negative vibrations spread across
the whole of this little planet. Of course, the same goes for when
good things happen, and sympathetic joy helps spread the positive
vibrations, precluding the arising of envy.

The Buddha advocated the cultivation of just four emotions, and
no others. These are called the *brahma vihāras*, or 'divine abodes'. The
first is a loving heart of unconditional love, the second is compassion,
the third is sympathetic joy (the positive counterpart of envy), and
out of these develops equanimity, the fourth and highest of the
emotions.

Self-addiction
The final fetter is – in a literal translation of the German *Selbstsucht*,
which I use to refer to this fetter – that of addiction to the self. We
are obsessed with this self of ours, or what purports to be the self.
We do not see any merits outside it, either in other people or in
situations it is unconcerned with. We are entirely focused on the
concerns of the self; and it is important to investigate how firmly
one's life is established in selfishness, and to realize how truly
difficult it makes daily life – that no positive result whatever can
come out of it. Selfishness blocks the possibility of any kind of
spiritual practice, leaving the ideal of unconditional love to remain
a hopeless fantasy. If the self is at the centre of things and there is
nothing as important, it is impossible to get rid of aversions because
anything that might threaten it, or provoke the fear of losing the
support it demands, will be repelled.

Selfishness is a constant, habitual attitude and very widespread:
all human beings assume for themselves great importance, and the
state of the whole world reflects this addiction to self. The difficulties
with which one struggles individually can likewise be traced back to
the self. Until one seriously contemplates this, one tends to imagine
that giving up ego-centredness will put one at a disadvantage, that
one must inevitably lose out. In fact, the opposite happens; it is the

way to get rid of our problems. This should really come as no surprise, for our customary behaviour and approach to life, based on an addiction to the self, leads us into endless trouble (let alone addiction to alcohol or other drugs). Our obsession with protecting the self and putting it at the centre of our activity is alone sufficient to make life difficult. It is the constant basis for friction and rancour between people, all with the same obsession.

Letting go of the self is possible only with the help of insight. It is not enough to say to oneself, 'Well, that sounds good – I will just go ahead and drop it, then.' Unfortunately it doesn't work like that. We need to practise letting go in everyday life as well as in meditation, bringing it to our every encounter. The entire spiritual path is one of letting go – that is, letting go *without* getting a replacement first. At the end of the journey, however, once we have let go of everything, the Buddha has promised us freedom, the end of suffering – a life free from clinging, free from aversion, free from wrong views, free from sceptical doubt, free from conceit, free from envy, and free from obsession with the self.

Living in such a way will also enable us to support the same journey in others. People who are searching for freedom themselves can often sense freedom of spirit in others, and are drawn towards it. This is the Buddha's teaching, and the opportunity to follow it is open to everyone.

There are four fundamental teachings, which are known to be authentic, age-old, handed down by ancient tradition. Their validity is unshaken now as in the past, and will remain unshaken. They are irrefutable to the wise, whether monk or lay. What are these four fundamental teachings? Cessation of craving is a fundamental teaching, known to be authentic,... cessation of hatred is a fundamental teaching,... right mindfulness is a fundamental teaching,... right concentration is a fundamental teaching....

Desires vanished, one shall rest,
No trace of anger in the heart;
With concentration and mindfulness within,
Composed in equilibrium.

Aṅguttara-Nikāya iv.29

9

Four Fundamental Teachings

IN THIS DISCOURSE the Buddha considers four fundamental principles: freedom from greed, freedom from hatred, right mindfulness, and right concentration. These four basic teachings, which are considered in a number of the Buddha's discourses, are sometimes called the four main themes of the spiritual life. When the Buddha says they are authentic, age-old, traditional, that they are as valid today as they were in the past, and that they will remain valid in the future, we can conclude that they are in no way peculiar to our particular religious community, and that their relevance is unaffected by any belief – or lack of belief – to which we might hold. Freedom from greed, freedom from hatred, mindfulness, and inner concentration are required for a balanced life, as for the spiritual path. And the Buddha's declaration that they will always be valid is of course as true today as it was 2,500 years ago; it is easy to see the truth of it. If we can recognize that they have a message for the past, present, and future, this may give us enough faith in the teaching to allow us to develop these fundamental states of mind within ourselves.

We already possess these four qualities. Their development means strengthening them sufficiently to tip the balance in their favour and overcome the frailties within us that tend to hinder them. The opposite of mindfulness is absent-mindedness, the opposite of inner concentration or composure is emotional instability, while non-greed and non-hatred are opposed, obviously, by craving and ill will. The more we foster what is wholesome and skilful within ourselves, the less easily can those unwholesome and unskilful factors arise within us, until one day we no longer experience them anywhere, and inner peace and tranquillity prevail.

Mindfulness

We will begin with mindfulness, since mindfulness stands at the beginning of any practice. Without mindfulness it is impossible to learn anything, let alone get to know oneself. We all employ mindfulness for everyday tasks like dialling the right telephone number, or putting enough stamps on an envelope. We also need mindfulness at work, in order to do our job as well as we can, for if we don't we'll probably be sacked!

This type of mindfulness is a necessity, as it is a basic requirement of life. It is effectively forced on us because there is simply no way of doing without it. We make use of it for the same reason as we work – mainly in order to survive. However, this mindfulness can be turned into a spiritual factor if we apply it to ourselves. We can start by observing ourselves dispassionately – and in this way get to understand ourselves – and on that basis make the necessary changes.

Mindfulness is a spiritual factor only when we apply it to ourselves, and this self-reflexive mindfulness is a most interesting undertaking. We will often need to be mindful of our environment – that is, to be aware of what is going on around us – but not in order to criticize or pass judgement, because being judgemental is a negative and reactive state of mind. Even when the world around us has to be the main focus of our attention, there are many situations in which we tend to react, and where we could benefit from more of an inner dimension to our mindfulness. For example, when we react to what someone has said, to how someone looks, to what someone does, mindfulness can make an enormous difference by contributing a clear picture of our inner life. Then it becomes all too obvious why there is no peace within us or around us. Everyone is caught up in their own reactions, at some times more than others, sometimes noisily, sometimes quietly. There are times when people swallow their reactions, while at others they let it all out. The results can be quite harmful, because negative thoughts and reactions are stored in the mind, where they become more firmly established, so the next time they surface even more quickly.

Mindfulness involves knowing these reactions and being aware that they do us no good. In fact, the person or situation that triggers our negativity is not harmed by it. We alone are damaged.

Mindfulness makes us aware of our emotional states and the objects of our thoughts, and allows us to turn negative emotions into positive ones. This is particularly the case if we can become aware of our emotional state before we get stuck in it. Once we are caught up in negativity it is much more difficult to extricate ourselves. It is important to regularly bring mindfulness to bear on our emotional states. A sombre mood often leads us to paint everything in dark colours, whereas in a bright and friendly mood the same events look totally different. This, of course, is how people form different perceptions of things. We are often puzzled that someone else does not find a situation as bad as we do, and conclude that they don't have any discrimination or intelligence, when it may well be that it is their emotional state that distinguishes their response from ours.

Most important for spiritual practice is mindfulness of the body, which involves being aware of our physical postures and movements. It should be relatively easy to practise it, for the body is visible and tangible, while emotional states and thought processes remain invisible and can only be experienced as they pass through the mind. Mindfulness of the body is necessary simply for survival, but we also make certain regular unconscious movements that can reveal a lot about us. If we observe ourselves carefully enough – how we move, stand, sit, and lie down – we start to know our body language, and the way it expresses our thoughts and emotions, and we will be able, if necessary, to make it more skilful.

Not the least reason to be mindful of the body in our daily tasks is that we otherwise risk cutting our finger, tripping on the stairs, or hitting our head. If we are not faced with these dangers, we won't pay attention, until an incident occurs that we afterwards regret. Even then we may not learn insight into ourselves, apart from the subliminal 'so that's how I am'. If we can adopt the vantage point of an observer on our behaviour, however, we should be able to assess what changes are necessary and possible.

Naturally, it is a lot easier to read the characteristic actions of others than to catch one's own body language. Indeed, this is how we make our most accurate assessments of people. We find it easier to understand someone from the message of what they do than from the meaning of what they say. It can often happen that someone speaks the right words, but they do not sound convincing. And this is because when body and speech are not in harmony we can sense it – we feel the body expresses something different from the words. Clearly, such an observation of others can help to illuminate similar discrepancies between our own words and postures, and in this way contribute to our understanding of ourselves. Dispassionate observation of this kind is neither judgemental nor critical. It's simply a way to learn from others what behaviour is helpful and what is not.

We can practise mindfulness on four levels: the physical body, feelings or sensations, emotional states, and thoughts (though these levels are interdependent, and not really separable). These four levels are traditionally known as the four foundations of mindfulness. Mindfulness of the body we have already looked at. Mindfulness of feelings involves being aware whether experiences are pleasant, unpleasant, or neutral. This primarily means bodily sensations, but the emotions are also involved, and these can lead to very powerful reactions in terms of our thoughts about our experience. Unpleasant or painful bodily sensations, say, may well be accompanied by a bad mood and corresponding reactive mental processes. In this way we can see that sensations, emotions, and mental processes work together.

Emotional states are more difficult to recognize than the mental reactions that form the content of our thoughts. It does not really matter which of these four foundations of mindfulness we take up, but we need to focus on one of them if we are to get to know ourselves, for it is only by knowing ourselves that we know what happens in the world. Once we have made ourselves the object of our inquiry it becomes clear that the world about us, other people, and ourselves, all have the same essential characteristics.

Successful scientific research may bring more knowledge, but that is all; it does not bring inner peace. By contrast, research into ourselves may not increase the sum of our knowledge but it will augment our wisdom and bring peace. It is for this task that we need right mindfulness. We will get to know one of the six billion human beings on earth and realize that under all the external differences we all look pretty much the same. We will also discover what things are truly helpful to us, and what things can only bring about our downfall.

The Buddha always regarded mindfulness to lie at the heart of the spiritual life, because it is through mindfulness that we can understand the world and ourselves according to how they really are. We are all familiar with the level of reality on which everyone appears to be a separate entity, each focused on having what they like; the level on which one identifies oneself with those people close to one, with one's possessions and with one's work, and within which we live isolated from others and from our environment. On this level there can never be any peace, for everyone is their own little kingdom, which is not to be invaded. But through practising mindfulness we can recognize that in reality we are all interrelated and form one totality, that, indeed, we cannot exist any other way. We all breathe the same air, and die without it; we share all sorts of essential conditions for our existence, including dependence on each other. Mindfulness teaches us that our bodies and minds get us into difficulties, and that it is the same for all other beings. In this way we will strengthen the sense of solidarity with all beings that is so important is easing our difficulties.

Non-hatred
The other teachings the Buddha regarded as fundamental to the spiritual life are those of non-greed and non-hatred. No one would question the desirability of these qualities, but some people think that hatred is an appropriate response to what is bad. Like most of our views, this idea, however widespread, is utterly wrong. According to the Buddha, we can only attain freedom by ultimately letting go of views altogether, and substituting the truth of understood experience.

Hatred for what is bad cannot reduce the amount of negativity in the world. It will simply increase the hatred within ourselves and make us worse. This adds to the general pool of hatred on our planet and multiplies our problems, be they at home, at work, or between countries.

Hatred in any form is emotionally draining because it continually dispels our peace. Many people never get to the point of actually starting to reduce their hatred because they take the view that they are entitled to hate whatever offends them. They have identified themselves completely with the things they consider to be right, and feel free to vent their hatred on whatever they regard as wrong, with the inevitable result that there can be no peace either within their minds or in the world around them. On the contrary, there can only be an eternal tug-of-war in the heart between approval and condemnation. The Buddha has said this himself, that hatred can never be overcome by hatred, only by love.

Truly to love that which is experienced as bad is a great challenge. We can make a start by asking ourselves – when we feel angry or resentful, filled with hatred or contempt – do we achieve anything positive by these feelings? This is the initial step, for which mindfulness is needed. Whether our aversion is justified is not the point; what matters is how we feel inside. Once we have learned to be aware of the feelings of hatred or bitterness in ourselves a few times, we come to realize that the state of mind connected with such feelings is not very pleasant. At some point arises the question 'What is it all for? Why should I make my life difficult with these negative feelings?' After all, the person we detest, despise, or find obnoxious usually does not know very much about our feelings. Most of the time these feelings remain as thoughts because we want to avoid the tensions, arguments, or open conflicts that might result from verbalizing them.

When at some stage we gain insight, we will realize the extent to which ill will produces bleak and unquiet states of mind, blocking any uplifting or joyful feelings, and how anger can turn into frenzy, generating terrifying emotional heat and making people crimson with fury.

If we want to change we have to see that we alone have created our inner life, that no one else is responsible. For that, we need to be able to spot our anger, hatred, or cold indifference as they arise, understanding that they are not helping to make us happy. If we are doing this, we probably also know that we should go on to 'cultivate the opposite' – as the Buddha puts it – even though the task of replacing hatred or callousness with loving-kindness is not an easy one.

The key component of this whole sequence is to understand that these negative feelings hurt us. The more hatred and anger present within us, the more difficult life gets, and the less connected with other people we feel. However, the one great advantage of these states of mind – if they are accompanied by some awareness – is that their pain makes us really want to change something. People who carry a lot of hatred are more likely to take up a spiritual path, because they experience so little inner peace.

It is important at this stage to understand that it is by working on ourselves that the most profound change can be made. This change may not get the whole world sorted out – neither the Buddha nor Jesus of Nazareth managed that. The world today looks very different from 2,500 or 2,000 years ago. The population has increased and there have been huge technological advances. But our predicament as individuals is fundamentally the same because hatred, war, and misery continue as always. We cannot make the world better, but we can make ourselves better as individuals, and this remains the best we can do for the world.

So it is no use reproaching other people or accusing them of irresponsible behaviour. By making peace within ourselves we will achieve more peace on earth, by at least one person, while also having an effect on the people we encounter – an effect that is entirely dependent on the strength and stability of that inner peace. Once we know it is up to us, that it is our responsibility, and we have decided we don't want to carry on living as before, we discover a natural inclination to check our surges of emotion by bringing more awareness into our feelings, and in this way become free from inner resistance and conflict. We see that we feel hatred because we are unable to get something we would like, we see that we become angry because we get something we don't like, and we also see that this resistance to our experience can be brought to an end.

With the help of mindfulness and the Buddha's suggested procedures for getting to know ourselves, we are in a position to start cultivating the opposite of those negative emotions. It is difficult to turn hatred into love, but at least we can try to replace hatred with compassion. If someone gives us problems we can first of all recognize that they have to deal with just as many problems as ourselves. We can bear in mind that this person is ultimately no different from us and that the separation is only apparent. One has only to make some contact with others to realize that we are connected on a deeper level. Another person instantly shares our experience of ourself when we talk to them, look at them, or simply share the same space. At the same time, we can have no idea what they might have experienced – what grief and sorrow, for example – so to regard them as someone outside our concerns, or think they are not as good as us, is completely inappropriate. This is true on all levels, be it that of the family, the nation, or the whole world. Being human means to know within ourselves all the good and all the bad. Living spiritually means developing and strengthening the good so that the bad recedes into the background. Perhaps nine out of ten people live according to the principle of being pleased with the good in themselves and justify the bad by finding someone else to take the blame, but someone who wants to take the spiritual path must go by a very different route indeed.

There are various methods for cultivating non-hatred. The most obvious is the loving-kindness meditation – the *mettā bhāvanā*, which can certainly make a very significant contribution to the development of a more positive attitude. It is not enough on its own, though, and daily life offers plenty of opportunities to continue the practice by means of friendly and loving behaviour. A feeling of equality in our basic humanity, of connectedness, love, and friendship, can only be developed by cultivating it in all situations. For instance, we can develop it towards people we know very little, with whom we have a neutral relationship in the activities of day-to-day life. We need to remind ourselves of our aim every moment of the day, because the mind is very forgetful. This again is mindfulness – to remember to practise.

We can all choose what we would like to know more about but, unfortunately, we are rarely curious about what goes on within ourselves. Only through mindfulness do we start to recognize how we relate to people in the course of everyday life – whether on coolly neutral terms, with animosity, or with friendliness. It is a never-ending, full-time exercise to generate accepting and loving responses to others, but it is a necessary one. Even when we simply can't stand someone, we must give up any notion of justifying our feelings. It is important at some stage to understand clearly and comprehensively that if we hold on to that notion we will not be able to change anything. Hatred exists, but there is no justification for it. It is a human weakness that we choose to live with, that we can do without, and that we can transform into our strength, which is love.

Non-greed

Predominantly greedy people are not as easily encouraged to practise as those given to anger, because they generally feel much happier. Greed is not as unsettling for our inner life as hatred. It is only periodically unpleasant: for example, when we don't get what we want – though if this happens too often, greed can turn into hatred towards the situation or people who deny us satisfaction. Apart from that, people who are driven largely by greed tend to have an easier time of it, because they can achieve a level of satisfaction relatively easily, being geared to experience straightforward pleasure. The result can be a lower degree of awareness of suffering, and therefore a lower degree of commitment to their practice, than those dominated by hatred. At the same time, the greedy type of person often finds their practice more rewarding. So we can conclude that in this respect both 'hate types' and 'greed types' have advantages and disadvantages.

Freedom from craving is an ideal of profound significance. On a basic level, craving is egotism: we focus on what we want for ourselves and arrange our own life to be pleasant and comfortable, while ignoring the needs of others even when we are in a position to offer help. At a more deep-seated level exists what in Buddhist terminology is called 'craving for existence', which repeatedly brings us back to the world through rebirth. This most powerful of all drives – the will to live – is a form of craving that underlies our fear of death. We fear the loss of existence in our present form. We may have ideas about what comes after, but the body with which we identify ourselves will disintegrate. This craving for existence is the fundamental drive behind hatred as well as all other desires.

Of course craving is not just about wanting to be here. We want to be something more than a physical body, we want to be someone, we want to be recognized, loved, and supported by people we know – and we want to be beautiful, or intelligent, successful, rich, or famous. But whatever it is we want to be, it is always just that – wanting to be: it all comes down to craving for existence. Short of Enlightenment, all human beings have this urge, and the more strongly developed it is, the more determined we are to satisfy it.

We might try to buy ourselves a sense of our own value: to be worth something in terms of possessions. We might try to earn ourselves a sense of our value, and create it in terms of our work or career. Though we must be aware that this is not possible, we act as though it is, because these things do make us feel really present and alive, and give us a sense of our own existence through a temporary sense of being worth something.

The desire to exist carries a lot of restlessness with it. We all know how difficult it is to sit down on our own, to calm down and do nothing – just being there without thinking, reacting, reading, or writing, without television, radio, or telephone – and it is because no one is there to assert that we are someone. This is the real reason for that restlessness, forcing us to do something – anything. At the same time we can always find some perfectly respectable reason to do things: we will never see an end to responsibilities and tasks, every day brings new things to do, so that it becomes impossible ever to finish it all.

Naturally, then, and unfortunately, this craving for existence disturbs our meditation too. Thoughts arise in order to confirm that we are here. The very moment thinking stops, anxiety, even fear, arises – 'Where am I if I do not think?' – and in no time at all new trains of thought are formed. Everyone new to meditation knows how difficult it is to slip into a tranquillity in which nothing happens and no self-affirmation is expected, for all our desires are ultimately built on this wish to be confirmed, to embody something.

The way to promote non-greed is to examine our thoughts and see whether they are overwhelmingly concerned with ourselves, or whether they also include others, near and far. Non-greed will develop to the extent that we take the 'you' element of our experience into consideration, alongside the 'me'.

Non-greed arises in parallel with generosity, the joy of giving. Generosity can actually be learned, and once we are practised in it we are always happy to find opportunities to give without a thought of receiving anything in return. Once giving becomes second nature, the barriers between 'me' and 'you' disappear, or at least diminish. After all, if we make someone happy, we bring some joy into the world, and we ourselves can enjoy it as well. It is a very common but totally mistaken idea that our joy can come only from what gives joy to us. What a miserable world that would be. The question to ask ourselves is, 'In what do I truly take joy, and how much of that joy can I pass on?' That true joy is the way we increase the joy in the world.

Whether it is a neighbour or people far away who experience joy, it always has a positive effect on us. Just as we breathe the same air, we all partake in a universal consciousness, in which joy, happiness, greed, non-greed, hatred, and love all leave their mark. So the better our ability to kindle positive emotion in ourselves and pass it on, the better the state of our world.

Composure and Concentration

The fourth of the fundamental teachings is composure and concentration. Right composure of the mind (*sammā samādhi* in Pāli) is meditation in its fullness, and working towards this involves one-pointedness of the mind, a focus on one thing. The mind we know in daily life constantly jumps from one thought to the next, and regrettably it does the same when we start to practise meditation, because for years and years it has been used for discursive thinking, and it cannot immediately extricate itself from that habit. But if we supply it with a regular opportunity to calm down, the mind gradually succeeds in becoming still. Finding the point where thought comes to a halt and we just rest in ourselves is a marvellous experience. Anyone who has ever experienced it knows how joyful it is. It sounds difficult to people who have never practised meditation, but everyone is capable of it. The teachings of the Buddha were not meant for spiritual geniuses but for ordinary people, for us. We, too, can learn to concentrate.

However, we need to practise daily in order to achieve results. The body can only remain supple with regular training, and the same is true of the mind. Generally, we understand training the mind as hard, concentrated thought. This is very tiring, as anyone who has a job that requires a lot of thought would agree. But thought is a function of the mind that can never lead us to its deepest dimensions; we cannot experience the truth of things by way of thought. This only becomes possible by way of meditation – 'by way of' because the experience of meditation is not the goal of Buddhist practice, but an important step on the way, because we cannot think the Absolute – we can only experience it. Whether we do encounter it, or just find deep tranquillity, in our meditation, we can come to understand that the satisfaction we have tried to find in the world actually lies within us. From our own experience we know that we cannot get happiness from other people, because they too are searching for happiness. It is only through meditation that we progress towards an experience of joy, satisfaction, serenity, and the absolute as present within us.

Composure of the mind begins with turning towards a meditation object, and the breath is particularly suitable for this purpose, because it is entirely neutral: everyone needs it for survival and it has a spontaneous movement upon which the mind can settle. We can also drop in a word – for example, 'peace' – so that the mind has something to do. Thus we say to ourselves 'peace' when breathing in, and 'peace' when breathing out. After sustained practice it will be possible to stay with the breath, not perhaps for hours on end, but long enough to suspend the thought process and to take a step into the deep. Then we cross a threshold and enter the inner chambers of the mind.

At the beginning of every meditation session it is very important to be aware of the fourth foundation of mindfulness – the objects of our thoughts – and to consciously label them appropriately. We will then realize that most thoughts revolve around the past or the future, and we tend not to live in the here and now, but constantly brood over what has been or dream over what might be. We become aware that such thinking cannot be real life, that it is no more than clinging to the past or hoping for the future. We come to understand that it is impossible to predict the future or alter the past and that therefore it is best to live our life in the present. Living is something we can do only in this one moment.

In meditation we can experience only the present breath; it is impossible to focus on the previous one or the breath to follow. When we start directing mindfulness towards the present in this way, we will become aware of the meaning of mindfulness. What will happen in the future or what occurred in the past will become uninteresting. If we recognize deeply enough that we really live only in this very moment we will try to be awake every moment of our life. When it comes to meditation, this means that we observe every breath, but we also notice our distractions and label them.

Thus we are already practising two of the foundations of mindfulness: mindfulness of the body (the breathing process) and mindfulness of the objects of our thoughts (distractions). This will enable us to continue our practice throughout the day, because regular training in mindfulness leads towards right composure of mind, allowing us to see the world in a totally different light. The 'me' is no longer seen as separate or as the centre of everything that happens; instead, a whole new world of unseen dimensions and beauty opens up.

Above all, we will be able to see absolute truth in clear contradistinction from relative truths – such as our belief that each individual sits on his or her meditation cushion with his or her own thoughts.

Right composure, or right concentration, is, like non-greed and non-hatred, a result of right mindfulness. The more awareness we develop, and the deeper our reflexive consciousness, the easier the practice of the spiritual life will become. We should not think we must get everything right immediately, just because we have formed the intention to practise. It is a way of life we have to follow every day, step by step, making gradual progress. Later, when we look back, we will see that both the inner person and the outer person have changed. On the outside we have grown older, while on the inside much is transformed and renewed. The words we employ may have remained the same but a new experience of life has arisen. By now it should be clear that the four fundamental teachings of non-greed, non-hatred, right mindfulness, and right concentration are vital at all times, in any religion, and for any type of spiritual path.

Whoever has clearly realized that peace of mind
Is their goal in life
Should work towards such disposition:
Being strong, upright, and conscientious,
Friendly, gentle, without pride.
Modest be they and easily content,
Not busy but frugal in their ways.
The senses calm, with clear understanding,
Not brazen or greedy in their behaviour.
Not in the smallest do they transgress
So that the wise could find blame.
May all beings be happy and find peace.
Whatever there is of living beings:
Be they strong or frail, big or small,
Visible or invisible, nearby or far away,
Already born or approaching birth,
May they all be happy.
May no one deceive or despise another
Out of anger or ill will,
No suffering wished on anyone.
As a mother with all her life
Protects her only child and keeps it safe,
So may one awaken for all beings and the entire world
An infinitely loving heart:
Free from hate, free from hostility, no boundaries
Above, below, in all directions.
Whilst walking or whilst standing, sitting or lying down,
With keen vigour may one develop this disposition:
'Heavenly abiding' it is called.
Not drowning in viewpoints,
Gaining virtue and insight,
Without attachment to sensual pleasures:
For those no more birth will be.

Mettā Sutta, Sutta Nipāta i.8

10

Loving-Kindness

THE DISCOURSE ON Loving-Kindness – *Karanīya-mettā-sutta* in Pāli – is one of the best known of the Buddha's discourses. It comes from the oldest part of the Pāli Canon, the Sutta Nipāta, which is considered by all scholars as the authentic word of the Buddha.

This brief and lucid discourse is concerned with the three parts of the Buddha's teaching, known in Pāli as *sīla*, *samādhi*, and *paññā*, and in English, generally, as ethics, meditation, and wisdom. In the Buddha's terminology wisdom is synonymous with insight and always refers to absolute or transcendental truth, so this sutta shows us the way from ordinary human life to the transcendental level of realization. It does this in terms of love: in this sutta we hear about a feeling with regard to all human beings, a feeling described as like that of a mother. Motherhood is a metaphor that characterizes an emotional life full of love, irrespective of whether it is that of a man or a woman.

Sutta means 'teaching discourse', *mettā* is 'loving-kindness' and *karanīya* is something like 'know-how'. The Buddha does not merely talk about how things should be; he shows us what methods to use. Actually, we all know how the world should be: no war, no conflict, love and happiness among people…. We have these wonderful ideas at our fingertips; the question is how to realize them. This is the key issue – how to put these ideas into practice – and that is why this discourse is called *karanīya*, how to do it. In Pāli the text is in verse, but I will set it out in prose.

Whoever has clearly realized that peace of mind is their goal in life should work towards such disposition.

Is peace of mind really the goal of our life? Are we, in fact, at all clear about our goal in life? Do we want to earn a lot of money or prestige? Do we want to become rich and famous? Do we perhaps want simply to find things interesting? Or do we want peace of mind? What are we searching for, honestly? Is it that we would rather fulfil all our material dreams and then have peace of mind in addition? Is that possible? It is utterly crucial to find out for oneself what is the most important thing in life. If we still think we can do whatever we fancy and that peace of mind will somehow just happen, it is time we woke up.

Of course, peace also means the end of war, and perhaps we believe that one day everyone will enjoy peace. However, this Utopian dream will not come true unless we begin with ourselves. Peace in the hearts of human beings means something totally different from political peace. If the people of the world had peace in their hearts, they would never shoot each other dead. Real peace can only evolve within ourselves and is the result of personal effort.

An interesting point is made in this first sentence of the sutta: a peaceful mind does not come about spontaneously. Inner peace requires an effort directed at a certain inner attitude. Sometimes the idea of a peaceful mind is taken to mean an attitude of not bothering about things. Yet just to practise meditation requires a fair amount of work. If we try to acquire some peace by separating ourselves from people, we shall find not peace but a feeling of indifference that can easily become cynicism. Inner peace is active and responsive: it is a direction of mind that aspires to the highest ideals. The primary lesson to learn from this discourse (as indeed from all Buddhist discourses) is that we should place this goal of inner peace at the top of our agenda. This doesn't necessarily mean having to adopt a quietistic way of life. It's not that we have to give up our job before we commit ourselves to the goal. We can be outwardly active and entirely peaceful inside – as long, that is, as we really know which inner attitude is conducive to it.

Being strong, upright, and conscientious,

Being upright means being sincere, honest, not chasing after our own advantage. It means being truthful – which is more than just not telling lies. Somehow we can always find an excuse for saying or doing something dishonest or insincere: we tell ourselves that it seemed the best policy, or it caused the least offence at the time. But our words should be entirely truthful: our outward expression should reflect how we think and feel inside. Our words should come from the heart, not just from the rational faculty, for if we let our heart speak we express our feelings, and this core of truth will always come through in what we say. Only speech that comes from the heart carries the truth. Someone else may have a different truth, but when they express it from their own heart, and you do the same, the result is what in the suttas is sometimes called 'noble' conversation. Such communication is said to be noble because it helps us to recognize ourselves more. As long as we talk only in logical, intellectual, or theoretical terms about our ideas, hopes, and purposes, we have not even touched our inner truth.

This is one aspect of reality. If we really want to experience peace in our mind we need to search for an absolute truth, one that is true always, not just in selected moments. Absolute truth is universal and all-encompassing, and can be realized only on the spiritual path. In order to recognize this truth we have to be able to meditate free from thought. Thought is very useful for earning a living, reading the newspaper, and also possibly for inventing something; but it is insufficient for understanding absolute truth. Our thinking is based so often on our notion of the ego: 'I' think! We do not need to spend very long talking to people about what we think and what they think to see that everyone thinks differently, even in a small group. How, then, could absolute truth be expressed through the exercise of thought?

In place of thinking, we have to learn through meditation to experience our inner life. On this basis we will come to a more universal view of ourselves and the world. As our way of looking at things changes, everything will look totally different.

Thus there are two directions to the value represented by the word upright: on the one hand it refers to the truth that comes from our heart and lets us encounter other people; on the other hand it refers to the absolute truth that we seek. This is not to say that all thinking has to be switched off while we search for absolute truth, but the way towards absolute truth is one of experience and understanding our experience.

Another inner quality specified in the text is conscientiousness. Being conscientious means that others can rely on us: we are reliable when we keep our promises or our appointments, when we take responsibility for our thought, speech, and action; in short, when we accept our karma. If it is clear to us that we are responsible for all we think, say, and do, we have understood what it means being the owner of our karma. If we still believe other people are responsible for what we think, say, and do, we have not yet embarked upon the spiritual path. Indeed, in trying to be our own best friend, we end up being our own worst enemy. As long as we are unable to monitor our thoughts in daily life and continue to allow negativity to arise, we will continue to make ourselves unhappy. If we believe something is someone else's fault, we have lost the game. We all know what conscientiousness means in ordinary life: working diligently, making accurate notes, and fulfilling our obligations to the letter. In the spiritual life it stands for much more: it means being responsible for oneself.

As for strength, this comes from putting in effort. It also represents our store of energy and resilience, both mental and physical. As a spiritual quality strength is a measure of our mental energy. It is the work we are able to put into our inner development. Peace and happiness can be experienced only through our own efforts, and there is no work that brings more happiness and meaning into our lives than the work we do on ourselves, on our own minds.

What we are up against is mental torpor, which is addressed in meditation as a hindrance to concentration. The mind has a natural inclination to become slack. It is easier for the body to slide downhill than to climb uphill, and the mental equivalent is just as true. The Buddha said that nothing stands still in the universe, and the same goes for ourselves: we go upwards or downwards but never stand still. Everything is in constant motion, whether we notice it or not. The Earth, for example, continuously rotates on its axis, even though we have no sense of that movement. Likewise we may not notice ourselves going downhill, but that is what happens if we let our practice slip and don't care about universal truths. With a strong and energetic mind, on the other hand, we can, in our daily life, investigate our thoughts and feelings, and use the ability to label them –

something we learn in meditation – to recognize clearly on which level of consciousness we are, and whether we are on the right path.

Thought is the cause of all that happens: we cannot say or do anything we have not prepared for in our minds beforehand, but we do not usually become aware of the thought because we react so quickly to it. In view of this, we need to work towards an energetic mind, a mind that searches for spiritual truth instead of pursuing sensual pleasure and easy comfort.

Friendly, gentle, without pride.

When looking at pride we need to distinguish between worldly and spiritual pride. Worldly pride is the vanity derived from our achievements, our position, our abilities. Spiritual pride means thinking we know it all because we have read or heard the teaching and grasped it intellectually. Such an attitude gets us nowhere: we have to practise the Dhamma. It is better not to have read it in the first place if all we develop is spiritual pride.

A certain satisfaction with our abilities can be skilful, but the pride that suggests to us we have more knowledge or ability than other people serves only to leave us even more separate from others than before. If we relate in this way, the language of the heart is suppressed because we are coming only from the logical intellect which is often devoid of the qualities of the heart. This is why spiritual pride impedes those who have acquired a lot of knowledge. Wisdom and knowledge are not the same, and speech dominated by intellectual knowledge hardly ever contains wisdom. Knowledge is helpful only if it can be put into action. Think a bit less and act a bit more! Teresa of Ávila said, 'Stop thinking so much; start loving more!'

The first step to wisdom is the hearing of information, the second is the development of knowledge, and the third step is the one that makes all the difference: the transformation of negative states into positive ones, the experience of the universal nature of everything, the experience of levels of consciousness that have a quality different from the usual market-place reality in which we live. Wisdom is the ability to understand such experience. The distinction between knowledge and wisdom is often misunderstood – as are the consequences of that misunderstanding. Make no mistake about it – it is we who have to live with those consequences, just as we will be the first to benefit from the awareness of the difference. Helping others by relaying information is very good, but wisdom cannot be passed on – everyone has to develop it for themselves.

As for gentleness, this is a pliability of the heart. The Buddha likened the quality of gentleness to bamboo in the wind. In a storm the bamboo bends right to the ground it but doesn't break, and when the wind subsides it straightens up again. So gentleness means being prepared to give way, not arguing, not trying to be right, not feeling we want to convince others, not demonstrating our superior knowledge, yet not allowing ourselves to be thrown off course. Pliability of the heart is a kind of giving. It is generosity of the heart, an offering of the heart. A hard heart cannot give itself, it is stuck in itself, surrounded by walls. Only a soft, yielding heart can give itself. Such a disposition leads to the boundless love that is *mettā*.

Friendliness doesn't mean dealing with others on a superficial level, saying yes all the time and telling others what they want to hear so as to suggest friendliness. Rather, it means communicating from the heart, through recognizing that we are all fundamentally the same, our differences only apparent. Friendliness from the heart demonstrates understanding of the universal nature of being, of all human beings and everything that surrounds us.

All existence is subject to dukkha, to difficulty. It is difficult to be human, and even more difficult to be a good human being. If we have recognized dukkha in ourselves we will recognize it in others. Then friendliness will no longer be mere politeness, but something real that comes from the heart.

Modest be they and easily content, not busy but frugal in their ways.

Being modest and easily content are not highly regarded in our society, because our entire economy depends on our not being modest in our demands. The more modest we are, the less we support consumerism. If we are easily contented we fail to boost the economy. Simplicity is virtually unknown in affluent societies, and to that extent so is fulfilment. Fulfilment in the world is impossible because our possessions break down, they have to be cleaned or renewed – or insured if they are very valuable – and we are constantly afraid of losing them.

True modesty is not common in poorer societies either, because people do not have the opportunity to live immodestly. So although the values of an affluent society may not be helpful, it is probably easier to be modest here, because we have the opportunity to try everything and recognize that whatever it is that the market place offers, it is not peace. It was as a prince surrounded by luxury that the Buddha-to-be was able to give up everything. It is easier to renounce something when we have had the experience of its impermanence, its inability to provide the satisfaction it promises, and its lack of inherent substance, a solid centre. It is much more difficult to give up wanting something when one has never experienced it or possessed it. In our society we can live a simple life because we have found that what we thought would make us happy has the opposite effect, and the affluence for which we have laboured has brought happiness to very few.

Dukkha is an important term in the Buddha's teaching. It does not just mean suffering, it denotes everything unsatisfactory about existence. In other words, it is about unsatisfied desire. If we find ourselves on the eternal wheel of desire and its satisfaction, we will never attain peace of mind. The less satisfied we are with what we have, the more we want, and the more trouble we go to in order to try to satisfy those wants. But the more we satisfy our desires the more dissatisfied we become. The more we go outside ourselves in our search for satisfaction, the less we will find inside ourselves.

Conversely, the fewer things we want the fewer difficulties we will have. If we could be satisfied by little, we would not constantly be wanting something extra from worldly activity. The fewer our needs and wishes, the more fulfilment we will find, and the easier it will be to dedicate ourselves to the spiritual path and find inner peace. We cannot go in both directions at once. Although we have a body to look after, modesty and satisfaction with few worldly possessions helps us to realize peace of mind. The Buddha said there are only four necessities: food, a roof over one's head, sufficient clothing to protect us from the weather, and medicine. We might want to check what else we possess. If we have needs that go beyond the four basic necessities, we are looking for fulfilment in the world, and will have to put more effort into worldly activities.

The senses calm, with clear understanding,

In the briefest possible terms both types of meditation are mentioned here: tranquillity meditation (calm senses) and insight meditation (clear understanding). However, we could use the expression 'clear mind' equally well. If we really meditate we have to give up sense desire for that period. We cannot eat, drink, lie in bed, or seek other sense contacts at the same time as meditating; we can only do one or the other. If we calm the senses we can reach deep tranquillity in meditation. We will know then what tranquillity can mean and that there is nothing more important for us than stabilizing this inner stillness. Through the experience of utter stillness we also recognize that our sense contacts – sight, sound, smell, taste, touch, and thought (thought is a sixth form of sense contact in Buddhism) – are always explained by the mind. The eye can see only colour and form, the ear can hear only sound, and these impressions are processed in the mind. According to the way the mind processes them, reaction follows. So to calm the senses the first step in meditation is to stop thought. Every thought triggers a feeling, then a perception, and again a new thought: an endless cycle of which tranquillity and peace can never be a part. But if by concentration and true meditation we cease to look outside the mind with the senses, and cease to comment on everything that passes through our mind, we will experience what it means to have inner peace. Once we experience this peace we will know there is nothing more important for us to search for. Having learned through meditation how to awaken inner peace it will be possible to maintain some sense of it during daily life, and we will then know what is important and stop searching for satisfaction in worldly activity.

Then: 'with clear understanding'. As most of us consider ourselves to be intelligent, we assume our understanding to be lucid and clear. Sadly, this is quite wrong. The reasoning we apply on the worldly level is stained through and through by our ego-illusion, our belief that we are separate from everyone else and that we have some special 'self'. Bound by this illusion, our intelligence operates merely on the worldly level, but if we discard this illusion, we can function on a level beyond the mundane and reach universal truths.

We can attain clear understanding only when there is absolute stillness in our mind, when the flood of ideas and emotions has subsided. When we look at a windswept ocean we see only the waves, and our vision cannot penetrate beneath the surface, and it's the same when we look within ourselves. But once we have found true peace through meditation, we discover the entire universe within ourselves. We are the microcosm within the macrocosm; all we ever want to know we already have within ourselves. As the Buddha said, 'The entire universe, O monks, lies in this body and in this mind.' Clear understanding means recognizing the characteristics of the universe that we carry within us: impermanence, unsatisfactoriness (i.e., insufficiency and unfulfilment), and 'corelessness' (lack of inherent substance). Only when the mind is completely calm and satisfied, and no longer wants or seeks anything, do these come clearly to mind, as an inner realization. This is called insight – which is self-explanatory: seeing within.

Not brazen or greedy in their behaviour,

The greed of our mundane life makes it difficult to give up our desires. Here, greed does not mean wanting everything two or three times, to buy new cars all the time or eat a lot, but that we constantly look outside ourselves to fulfil our inner desires. On the spiritual level, greed means the desire for existence, not being able to accept the fact of inevitable death and regarding existence as absolutely important. This desire is accompanied by craving for non-existence, which manifests when things go wrong and we no longer want to be there, when we have had enough, or when want others to see what it's like trying to manage without us.

Once the desire for existence has become less dominant, we recognize that we can be much more flexible, that things are no longer so overwhelmingly important because being here is no longer so overwhelmingly important either. But giving up our life is not giving up on life, it doesn't mean committing suicide. Rather, the desire for non-existence is merely the flipside of the desire for existence. It means we know how impermanent we are. No one is guaranteed to be alive tomorrow or even arrive home this evening. We assume, we hope, we plan – but who knows whether we will still be alive next year? Let us surrender ourselves wholly for once, and recognize that we are totally impermanent! There is only this one moment: all others are already past or only a hope. The future does not exist because, when it comes to be, it is present. The past, like the future, exists only in our minds. Real experience is just this very moment when we are truly present and within which we can appreciate how ephemeral everything truly is. The only thing that matters is living this moment skilfully: full of love and generosity, dedicated, with a meek and accepting heart that knows that we are, all of us, in reality, one life. We have to realize that although it looks as though we are all separate, like individual units floating in the universe, this is just a trick of the mind, an optical illusion (an understanding of inter-relatedness that is now scientifically confirmed). We need to recognize once and for all that the desire for existence cannot be fulfilled – not ever. We are all on our way to the cemetery, it is only a question of time, and age is not the decisive factor. The only difference is that when we are old we no longer make the mistake of our youth and believe we will stay young forever.

The desire for existence drags everything else in its train: the desire to have and hold on to things, and to enjoy sensual pleasures. The desire for existence, the spiritual form of greed, gets us into trouble over and over again, perhaps with our never even becoming aware of it. Again, this is not to say we have got to die, but that we should acknowledge that we are here for only a short while, that we are guests on this earth, actors in a play. Even as we are putting on our costumes and making our first appearance, we start identifying with the part, believing we really are the person we are playing. We need things to belong to us in order to prove to ourselves that we really are this character and will remain so. The more we do this the more inflexible become our views. And this creates even more trouble from a spiritual perspective: our views are so ingrained that it takes a lot of effort to understand the context of our deeper connections, and to let go. As always, the key phrase is 'letting go'.

Not in the smallest do they transgress so that the wise could find blame.

This is a reference to the first precept: to do no harm. The practice of the precepts conduces to a life of harmony, with no pangs of conscience, and in peace. If we observe the precepts they can form a basis for peace in meditation. As we have seen, this discourse contains all three parts of the teaching: moral conduct as basic support, meditation to discover tranquillity, and the insight that arises from these conditions.

May all beings be happy and find peace.
Whatever there is of living beings:
Be they strong or frail, big or small,
Visible or invisible, nearby or far away,
Already born or approaching birth,
May they all be happy.
May no one deceive or despise another
Out of anger or ill will,
No suffering wished on anyone.
As a mother with all her life
Protects her only child and keeps it safe,
So may one awaken for all beings and the entire world
An infinitely loving heart.

In other words, we wish all people, without exception, that which we wish ourselves. The mother is presented here as a model of tender loving care. We may have seen mothers who are not such models, but in general mothers give themselves over to their children in a way their children cannot give to them. It should be noted that the feeling of protection and care a mother has for her only child is not the ideal in itself – it is only a metaphor for that ideal – and the Buddha goes on to say that we should develop such a feeling not towards just one child but towards all beings. This is particularly interesting for parents, who should compare the way they regard their children with the way they regard other people. The difference is huge, and we need gradually to reduce it. We are in a unique situation with regard to our children, but the Buddha said that everyone has at some time been our child, our mother, and our father. If we have no children we can direct our awareness towards how our mother relates to us and perhaps reflect that this special relationship, inasmuch as it results in clinging, is often not to the child's benefit. We should reflect in such ways to encourage ourselves to extend the feeling we have for our children, or our mother, beyond those boundaries. We should broaden the limits of our love, since we have all been in close relationship with each other before.

Why should we restrict ourselves to one or two people out of six billion? Since that is what we do, fear arises, fear that we will lose the people we love. And that spells an end to pure love, because fear is ultimately derived from hatred. This doesn't mean we hate our children; we hate the idea of losing them. But then the purity of our love is compromised, for true love can only be unconditional and limitless. We need to let go of the condition that we want those people to be here and to stay here with us. If we have children ourselves we are given an excellent personal perspective on the difference we assume between the importance of our children and the importance of others. We need to ask ourselves whether it would not be more skilful to drop the fear of losing our children and develop the same kind of love towards our neighbours. Maybe they don't look as cute, perhaps they are quite elderly, but what is the problem with that? The real problem is that they are not 'mine', yet they are 'my' neighbours, and they populate the same earth, breathe the same air, and use the same street as I do. They are 'mine' in the same way as everyone else.

What is mine? The body? That will end up at the cemetery, probably at the most inconvenient time we can imagine. What about the mind? If it is mine, why does it take us for a ride, play tricks on us, and make us unhappy? Are my children mine? They will certainly see it differently when they grow up. So, what is mine? 'Mine' only means we are here and feel part of this universal process to which we try to contribute the best we can offer.

We are all keen to avoid environmental pollution. The worst kind of pollution, however, consists in corrupting thought and cold-heartedness. Through developing loving-kindness we clean and protect the environment. If a kind-hearted attitude and compassionate behaviour became more widespread we would stop the pollution of our environment that results from cold-hearted attitudes.

We can reduce this enormous difference between interest in our children and interest in our neighbours by bringing awareness to the feeling for our children and transferring it to other people. They are all 'mine' because they are here at the same time, eat similar food, have the same needs, and all belong together, and every single one has some influence on our life.

Such a sense of wholeness helps us feel less separate or threatened, and we can therefore express less of the aggression, negativity, or cynicism that understandably follows from feelings of isolation and vulnerability. If the love we bear as a mother or father imparts to us a spirit of solidarity, based on the feeling that we are all human – at the same time and on the same planet – then this love has served its purpose. If, however, mother love is used only to raise children, it will miss the point. It is sufficient on the worldly level, but not on the spiritual plane where we can use this love as the seedbed for opening our heart and learning kindness. That is the Buddha's message, especially in this discourse.

> *Free from hate, free from hostility, no boundaries*
> *Above, below, in all directions.*
> *Whilst walking or whilst standing, sitting or lying down,*
> *With keen vigour may one develop this disposition:*
> *'Heavenly abiding' it is called.*
> *Not drowning in viewpoints,*
> *Gaining virtue and insight,*
> *Without attachment to sensual pleasures:*
> *For those no more birth will be.*

This is a description of Enlightenment. Our views and opinions are our greatest enemies, for we believe in them and they seem to belong to us. Because they are, so to speak, our views, they limit us because we cannot easily accept other opinions at the same time; they may even provoke hostility against those with different views. Since everyone has their own views, we can never coexist peacefully together. Identical views are very rare, whether about art, or philosophy, let alone about truth. As long as we hold to our personal views and believe in them absolutely we are separated from each other.

Views are intellectual explanations that are not based on understood experience. Understood experience is the foundation of the Buddha's discourses. It is the dawning of insight, and helps us along the way. Views always originate in the mundane consciousness and are the opposite of insights, which come from the heart. Therefore, if we want to investigate whether something is an insight or a view, we need to see whether the heart is involved or whether we have just thought it up. According to the Buddha, it is predominantly our views that prevent us from gaining insights.

We all have views, of course, but we do not have to believe in them. If we stop believing in them we are more open to other views; we may be able to say, 'Well, that view is also valid.' The harmful nature of all views is that again and again they lead to ego-illusion.

Then, virtue and insight. The basis for the spiritual path is virtue, ethical behaviour, but we do not have to bring virtue to perfection before we can meditate, otherwise all meditation classes might as well be cancelled. We work on all fronts: on virtue, on concentration, and on insight. We don't need to be perfect in one area in order to move on to the next.

'Without attachment to sensual pleasures' is a crucial point. We should prefer the spiritual to the worldly life and know our priorities. If we had a choice between meditation and drinking tea, or going on retreat and going skiing, we would, if we were not attached to sensual pleasures, always choose meditation. It might be that we enjoy sensual pleasures during the meditation class, too, but once on the spiritual level of experience we no longer search for sensual pleasures; we have already found an entirely different realm of experience within ourselves. With regard to any sense contact, we experience it much more purely and strongly, while losing any interest in hanging on to it or renewing it. That is, we are not distracted in any way from the unalloyed sense experience. Anyone who has been to a few meditation classes knows that after a concentrated session we perceive the green in nature as much greener, the blue as much bluer. The sense impressions get more intense and make a stronger impact, and because we want neither to cling to them nor repeat them, they are just impressions, pure and simple.

Being without attachment means one has changed one's priorities. What is really important? We generally only recognize what is important when we realize that all we have achieved so far has vanished into thin air. But we can realize the same thing from observing the impermanence of the subtlest sense-impressions. When we see that sense-impressions never stay with us, we become aware that seeking happiness through the senses might be not quite the right way after all. Most people never see it that way, but the Buddha said there are some people 'with little dust in their eyes' who will understand. The few who succeed in uncovering this insight have found a new way.

'No more birth' denotes Enlightenment. There is of course a lot that one could say on this topic, but all I would suggest here is that maybe we can recognize how our desires are reborn by the hour, even every minute. We want something new all the time. Now we go for a walk, then we want to sit down, then get up, then read a book, have a little nap, go into the garden – a constant cycle of desires. When someone has attained absolute insight, this rebirth of desire ceases.

By way of summary it may be said that this discourse first gives a detailed description of the dispositions or attitudes that we can make our own: everyone is free to adopt them. As a second step, meditation leads to clarity of the mind. Through right disposition or aspiration and clarity of the mind, the heart opens up, ready to give, progressively diminishing our views and sense desires, until one day perfect purity and insight arises.

A long time ago King Milinda
Left his capital city, Sāgala, and went
To visit Nāgasena, the monk,
As the Ganges flows to meet the sea.

When he arrived, the king asked questions
Of him, the teacher who had dispelled darkness
And kindled the flame of truth;
Many questions, deeply considered.

Likewise were the answers to these questions
Fruit of the most thorough and profound reflection;
Easing to the heart, pleasant to the ear,
They called forth awe and wonder.

Investigating the discipline and sublime doctrine,
Disentangling its complex layers and threads,
The monk's brilliant speech excelled
In parables and logical thought.

May you, too, direct your understanding here,
The heart joyful, overflowing, and buoyant,
And listen to these profound discourses,
Which destroy all grounds for doubt.

Milindapañha i.1

11

Gaining Insight

THE MILINDAPAÑHA records a dialogue between a king, Milinda, and Nāgasena, an eminent Buddhist monk. Milinda lived in the second century BCE, and was the descendant of a Greek ruler invested by Alexander the Great after his conquest of north-west India in the fourth century BCE. (His name translates the Greek 'Menandros'.) Although this work is not a canonical text, it is regarded as an important early example of Buddhist teaching after the *parinibbāna* (death of the Buddha), and is frequently quoted. It consists of a short introduction, given opposite, presenting the context of the teaching in the customary eulogistic manner, followed by seven chapters setting out a sequence of questions and answers, from which I shall consider just one, question 13 from chapter 2:

The king spoke thus to the Venerable Nāgasena: 'Lord, what is the essential characteristic of concentration?'

'Its defining characteristic is that it serves as the focus or leading edge of development, because all good qualities are drawn together by concentration; they have an inclination and a tendency towards it; they are focused upon it.'

'Help me to understand with a parable!'

'As the rafters of a gabled house all lead to the ridge, tend to the ridge, meet at the ridge, and as the ridge is therefore seen

*to be the most important feature of the building, so with all
good qualities; they have concentration as their focus or
leading edge, they are inclined towards it, tend towards it,
and they all come together in it.'*

'Give me another parable!'

*'As when a prince goes to battle with his fourfold army, all
his troops – elephants, horses, chariots, and archers – have
him as their leader; they look to him, take their direction
from him, and assemble round him. So with all good
qualities: they have concentration as their focus or leading
edge, they are inclined towards it, tend towards it, and they
all meet together in it. To this extent is right concentration a
focus and leading edge of development. Besides, the Exalted
One has said: "Practise concentration; he who is
concentrated sees all things as they really are."'*

'You are indeed most accomplished, Venerable Nāgasena!'*

The Buddha often spoke about concentration or meditation. In one
of his last discourses he said to a disciple:

*'These higher states of consciousness are not called renunciations in
the noble rule of the Order; they are regarded as states of bliss in the
noble rule of the Order.'*†

In the commentary we find a further explanation of this point:

*Those in the world who are eager to learn and practise this higher
state of consciousness with the intention of leaving it behind [i.e.
without clinging to it], aim to develop insight on the basis of
concentration. To them comes the bliss of insight through the
development of full concentration and even through the
development of access concentration, which is the way to the ending
of the mind's oppression. Therefore the Exalted One says, 'Train in*

---

* Milindapañha ii.1.13
† Majjhima-Nikāya i.40

*the development of concentration. He who is concentrated sees
whatever is as it really is.'*[*]

At this point a connection is made between concentration and rebirth:

*The development of concentration leads to higher states of existence.
Therefore, those worldlings [those who have not yet reached Stream
Entry or any of the subsequent grades of transcendental
purification] who keep practising concentration and who – whether
they desire rebirth in the Brahmā-world or not – do not suffer the
loss of their concentration, find through the development of
concentration the bliss of higher states of existence.*[†]

So a concentrated mind at least ensures a good rebirth. The Exalted
One therefore goes on:

*In such a way those who have developed the first absorption to a
certain degree are reborn among the devas of the retinue of Brahmā.
But even the development of access concentration leads to a higher
state of being within sense-based realms of existence.*[‡]

We can assume that this higher state refers to a better life in either
the human realm or the deva (god) realm.

*Those noble ones, however, who have reached the eight attainable
states and have developed concentration with the purpose of
entering the state of cessation, of attaining the release of nibbāna
even in this very lifetime, and dwelling there in happiness, they
find the bliss of cessation through the development of concentration.
Therefore the wise one does not forbear the ardent development of
concentration, which bestows manifold blessings, purified of the
defilement of desire.*[§]

There is also an interesting simile elsewhere in Buddhaghosa's
Visuddhimagga on how we may gradually bring the mind to concentration, and how we may recognize the concentrated mind:

[*] Visuddhimagga xi.121
[†] Visuddhimagga xi.122
[‡] Visuddhimagga xi.123
[§] Visuddhimagga xi.124

For this monk's mind which has pursued visible and invisible objects for a long time does not like to enter into concentrated mindfulness of in-breath and out-breath as object, just as a cart drawn by a young and stubborn bull strays from the way. Suppose a herdsman wishes to tame a stubborn young bull which has been nurtured on the milk of a stubborn cow. Such a one will lead the calf away from the cow and tie it to a heavy post fixed firmly into the ground nearby. And the young bull turning this way and that and unable to run away, will eventually sit or lie down beside this same post. Likewise, the monk who wishes to tame and master his mind that has been nurtured for long on the rich sustenance of visible and other objects and grown wild, may lead it away from visible and other objects, may go to the forest or some other secluded place, and in that place may tether it with the halter of mindfulness to the post of in-breath and out-breath. And his mind, turning this way and that, unable to find the objects to which it formerly attended, and unable to break the halter of mindfulness and run away, will eventually settle down beside this very object, in 'access' or full concentration. Therefore the masters of old say:

As you tie the calf you wish to tame
Firmly to the post,
So tie your own mind
Firmly to the mental object.[*]

This passage emphasizes on the one hand the importance of concentration, and on the other, how difficult it is to attain: it is as laborious as the taming of a wild bull. It also says something about the results that can be expected. Two kinds of concentration are mentioned: access concentration and full concentration. Some Burmese writings also refer to momentary concentration, which is something we have all had some experience of, as for example when we make a telephone call and have to concentrate on dialling the right number. This type of concentration is obviously not specifically linked to meditation, and is not considered by the Buddha in his teachings.

---

[*] Visuddhimagga viii.153–4

Access Concentration

Access concentration is the meditative state in which, although the attention is settled on the meditation object, thoughts still pass through like clouds at the back of the mind. So two things appear to be happening: concentration on the breath, and, simultaneously, shadowy thoughts whose content we cannot determine because they pass so quickly. In this case we need to apply more determination in order to direct the mind more assiduously towards the meditation object. However, we should try not to apply goal-oriented thinking. Being over-preoccupied with the achievement of concentration is counter-productive, as meditation is all about letting go. Access concentration does not take us into the meditative absorptions but it already has a different feeling from that of the completely distracted mind. A fully concentrated mind is one that is able to remain long enough with a meditation object (such as the breath, loving-kindness, or the contemplation of feeling) to gain entry to the meditative absorptions.

The Meditative Absorptions

Very few people are interested in the meditative absorptions, but these actually constitute the way of meditation, as the quotation from the *Visuddhimagga* makes clear. Other more contemplative methods of meditation lead in the direction of insight, but only the absorptions lead automatically to changes in our state of mind, giving us the clear vision of insight or wisdom. In fact, we have two directions of meditation, tranquillity and insight, and it is imperative to know the purpose of our training. The best guide will be useless if we don't know from where we are setting out, and the best techniques are useless if we don't understand their purpose. Meditation does not mean groping in the dark for haphazard results. On the contrary, it is a science – the science of the mind, and it is accessible to everyone, provided they have sufficient information and practise regularly. Meditation can reasonably be described as a science, because it has been described in specific terms, and its results are equally specific and repeatable; there is nothing random or fortuitous about them.

The Buddha himself described the results of meditation in terms of the absorptions clearly and precisely, albeit briefly. We will now consider the insights they are meant to convey, with the caveat that the Buddha's words are only pointers to the right path; we have to take every step on that path for ourselves.

The First Meditative Absorption

Taking the example of the mindfulness of breathing, we may say that the first meditative absorption is characterized by a more and more subtle experience of the breath, which might then become imperceptible, until a rapturous bodily feeling arises. The first absorption is characterized by five positive factors working against the five traditional 'hindrances' to meditation (sloth and torpor, doubt and indecision, hatred and ill will, restlessness and anxiety, and sense desire), and putting us through an automatic process of purification, like a kind of spiritual washing machine.

According to the Buddha, once we develop the first meditative absorption, even to a limited extent, we are guaranteed a good rebirth. It is quite reasonable not to be interested in a good rebirth for its own sake; indeed, to attain the first absorption in the course of this life is enough of a reward in itself. It is certainly an advance on whatever rebirth is to come.

The five factors making up the first absorption are: initial application to the meditation object (*vitakka*), persistent or sustained application (*vicāra*), rapture (*pīti*), joy (*sukha*), and one-pointedness (*ekaggatā*). One-pointedness is required not only for meditation but also for contemplation and insight methods of meditation, as without at least some degree of one-pointedness we cannot usefully work on anything. These five factors have an automatic effect on the five hindrances. Firstly, initial application (*vitakka*) – particularly in the form of an initial application of concentration – counteracts mental lethargy, a characteristic of sloth and torpor. Sustained application to the meditation object (*vicāra*) counteracts sceptical doubt, as it gives the mind a taste of deepening peace, but sceptical doubt is only entirely eradicated at the first nibbāna experience, traditionally known as Stream Entry.

Pīti, which consists in a rapturous physical sensation, counteracts ill will, inasmuch as we cannot experience ill will and rapturous joy simultaneously; and it also weakens ill will generally because we know we can sit down and experience that rapture again at any time. Indeed, the more often we develop *pīti*, the more thoroughly ill will is expelled, though it cannot yet be completely uprooted, because our hindrances and propensities can only be eradicated through insight, which is gained by expanded meditative awareness. *Sukha,* or blissful joy, counteracts restlessness and anxiety, for if we experience joy we need not look for anything else. Finally, one-pointedness (*ekaggatā*) counteracts sense desire. If we focus the mind one-pointedly on our meditation object we cannot plan, for example, what we are going to have for breakfast.

Thus the first absorption, which we experience as a sense of physical rapture, counteracts the five hindrances with a deeper level of experience, but its main significance is that it brings us on to the path of meditation.

The Second Meditative Absorption

During the first absorption, the sense of rapture is combined with blissful joy. When this rapture is left behind, we enter the second absorption and blissful joy is realized and savoured more fully as it becomes the single object of meditation.

Though blissful joy is a steadier experience than rapture, it is still impermanent, and we are missing the point of meditation if we get attached to the feelings it produces. Another thing to recognize is that joy normally comes through our sense contacts, through sight, sound, taste, smell, touch, or thought. Until now it has been dependent on external conditions – but in the second absorption we experience a joy that is dependent only upon our inner life, especially our concentration. Once we have understood that we do not need to rely on others for joy, our relationships with people will start to change: when they please us, that is certainly pleasant, but we no longer expect them to please us, or get upset when they don't. If this is not happening, we may have had the experience of joy, but not paid enough attention to its meaning in order to gain insight.

We can attain a further transformative insight regarding our attitude to sense contacts. Owing to the incomparably more intense joy of meditative absorption compared with anything we experience in mundane life, our sense contacts become less important, and we no longer constantly seek satisfaction through our sense contacts.

Human life at all times involves pleasant sense contacts, for there is beauty everywhere: to see, hear, smell, taste, touch, and think about. This is what makes life bearable. This insight does not mean we should not enjoy a beautiful sunset; it means rather that we realize, for one thing, how transitory are all our sense contacts (particularly obvious with a sunset, of course) and, for another, that the joy arising through any mere sense contact cannot be compared to the bliss of the second absorption. The bliss experienced in the second absorption is much purer and more overwhelming for not being based on sense contact, and for not being accompanied by clinging. Bliss can arise only when we have let go of the external world and found the way to our inner life. This still leaves us free to enjoy sense contacts, but without expecting complete and lasting fulfilment from them and no longer constantly looking for the enjoyable ones and getting attached to them.

Conversely, unpleasant sense contacts are no longer a cause for distress, because we know they will go away. After we have experienced the deeply penetrating bliss of the second absorption, we no longer need to react to unpleasant sense contacts – they only touch us so deeply because we react to them. Instead, we start to view them as mere phenomena that come and go, and because of this, because we have recognized their transitory nature, we neither cling to the pleasure they give us nor shrink from those that are unpleasant. This means we have a much purer access to each pleasant one as it occurs. If we do not seek it, want it, expect it, or get attached to it, we will pass through a moment of unspoilt joy, and not experience disappointment once it is over.

If we fail to become aware of such insights arising from the second absorption, we have not examined our experiences thoroughly enough when coming out of meditation. They need to be authentic realizations if they are to influence the quality of our life. It is not difficult for anyone who meditates to learn the absorptions. How long it takes us to become concentrated is just a question of time, but it depends also on karmic conditions. People with a strongly analytical mind, who want to contemplate and investigate everything, often need to gain insights before they can find stillness or peace. Generally, the easier way is to find stillness first and then insight, for the meditative absorptions automatically bring insights.

The Third Meditative Absorption

In the third meditative absorption we experience contentment, again recognizing cause and effect. Once we have concentrated for long enough on the meditation object, we gain access to the inner life.

Once we have experienced the delightful physical sensation for long enough, we find joy. Through a sustained feeling of joy, contentment arises because eventually finding the happiness and joy we have been looking for makes us content. This contentment leads to peace.

From the third absorption we can gain the insight that contentment is only possible as long as desires are absent. If we would like to have peace in our everyday life without trying to arrange all our external circumstances in such a way that *they* make us content (which is impossible anyway), we need to drop our wanting. With this insight we can experience peace.

As long as we want to change the things and people around us we are constantly in turmoil and discontented. The only human being we can change is ourselves. Others are only the backdrop to our lives, and if we are unhappy with them arguments and annoyances are not far away. One trouble follows the other. We think that our discontent is due to exterior things because we have not yet realized that they originate from within. The third absorption can make us realize that contentment is only possible while we harbour no desires. This leads to a feeling of resting in oneself and of inner strength.

Contentment from the third absorption can spread into everyday life. We are often irritated when we experience dissatisfaction and would like to find a scapegoat. At this point we should remind ourselves of its true cause. During the day we need to re-contact our insights from the absorptions time and again – if our spiritual practice happens merely on the cushion and is not carried any further or even forgotten, it will be of little use. Our only advantage then is that during meditation at least we feel well and get rid of the pain in our knee, but this is certainly not the reason for meditation.

The insights gained during the absorptions are not only consistent with reason, they also need to be experienced to be understood, and such experience needs to happen with each individual. It is best if these insights arise, not during the absorption, but when we come out of it. It is possible to gain them at the time of the absorptions but we would need to be very well trained and advanced in meditation to avoid being distracted. It is not therefore recommended when we start; rather, we need to go as far as we can with the absorption and when it comes to an end, recapitulate and ask ourselves, 'What have I experienced? What do I take out of it? Even this is impermanent. What have I learned?' Awareness and understanding of these experiences is the purpose of meditation. Because we have gone through it for ourselves we have received a deep-reaching training of the mind. There is no doubt in our own mind that these realizations are authentic, even if others may doubt. Our inner life changes in this way. Understood experience is the gateway for wisdom.

The Fourth Meditative Absorption

The first three absorptions are not very difficult to learn; the fourth, however, is more demanding. The first four are called the subtle body or fine-material absorptions. They still have substance and a similarity with certain states that we encounter in daily life, yet they have a different basis. In our daily life also we know delightful physical sensations, joy, and contentment, although not to such an extent and always reliant on external circumstances. In the fourth of the meditative absorptions the sense of peace deepens to absolute stillness. This experience becomes the meditation object and its recognition serves only to support it.

So in the first absorption the meditation object is the delightful bodily sensation, in the second absorption it is joy, in the third absorption contentment, and in the fourth stillness. Only the meditation object is present in the mind, nothing else. There can be some confusion about these characteristics of the absorptions. When we are learning to meditate, they sometimes flash past us and we touch them only momentarily. They become meditative absorptions only when we can sustain them, when there is nothing in the mind but the meditation object.

The stillness of the fourth absorption seems to go into greater depth, as if the mind is sinking, though of course it isn't – the mind is settled exactly where we put it. Just as when we focus our mind on our right big toe, it is there; so if we let our mind go into the depth of stillness, we will feel immersed in that stillness.

Once we experience this stillness we can see that such utter tranquillity is only possible if we abandon most of our ego-centredness. This insight paves the way for the desire for liberation. Every mature person seeks tranquillity, peace, and happiness. When we have discovered that this deep tranquillity is only possible once our ego-centredness has moved entirely into the background, we will have a stronger desire to give up ego-centredness and ego-illusion.

All this has to be experienced, not thought up. The absorptions can of course also be rather shallow. It can happen that we experience them deeply but the next time we are not sufficiently concentrated, and we experience some peace and joy but not so sweepingly. However, experience of the absorptions can be sufficiently potent to have a substantial and lasting impact. On a mundane level, when we fell in love for the first time it made a strong impact. The impact of the meditative absorptions has to be at least as profound as that for us to attain insights from the experience of the absorptions.

Together with the desire to relinquish ego-centredness emerges a wholehearted desire for the liberation expressed in the Buddha's teaching. We have already experienced for ourselves the truth of one of the Buddha's essential messages: that ego-illusion stands in the way of happiness. We receive, as it were, a taster of how it might be once we have dropped our ego-illusion. Through this realization and commitment to the Buddha's teaching, our faith develops. We do not think up what to do; we follow the Buddha's instructions with confidence and commitment.

The next thing we notice is the increasing urgency of our practice. Consequently, we practise right now, not postponing it until we have better conditions, better weather, or better friends. We start to feel the urgency, the desire for liberation and trust. It is only with faith, trust, and confidence that we are able to dedicate ourselves. We become like children who trustingly take their mother's hand to cross the road. The child completely trusts its mother, gives itself up to mother's wisdom, and follows mother's advice. If we let a child-like spirit return to us and don't claim to know everything ourselves or just follow our own impulses, we will succeed in dedicating ourselves trustingly to the Buddha's teaching. In most cases this becomes possible only once we have practised the fourth meditative absorption long enough and thoroughly enough. It also depends on our karmic conditions.

In the fourth meditative absorption the mind receives a massive energy boost. If we practise the fourth absorption regularly we grow much more clear-headed. It works almost like a mental fountain of youth. Just as the body goes to sleep at night and replenishes its energy, the mind gathers strength when it experiences the deep peace of the fourth absorption. A mind that wants truly to understand how things are correlated and connected needs such regeneration.

Beyond the First Four Meditative Absorptions

The fourth absorption is the springboard for the four formless absorptions. They are called formless because they have no substance. Although the impact of the first four absorptions is strong, the higher meditative absorptions have an even deeper impact. The fifth, sixth, and seventh absorptions are called *vipassanā jhānas* (*vipassanā*: insight, *jhāna*: meditative absorption), as they are particularly suitable for bringing forth insights. It is possible just to enjoy the first four absorptions and even reach the conclusion that we are brilliant meditators and pat ourselves on the back. This is impossible in the fifth, sixth, and seventh absorptions, for a mind that is awake and aware enough to reach these heights also gains the insights associated with them.

Through these absorptions it is possible to acquire abilities that we might call supernatural. However, that is just what they are not. The mental faculties obtained by someone who practises the *jhānas* were deliberately not explained by the Buddha, and he warned us not to dwell on them until we are Enlightened.

Insight in the Formless Meditative Absorptions

Grasping for the insights that originate in the formless absorptions is not the same as will-power. Will-power gives us the energy to achieve what we set out to do, but its function is not to enable us to imagine what we want to achieve, since this result orientation prevents us from really living the spiritual life. Many people have a problem with this distinction and do not understand the difference between will-power and result orientation. If we are focusing on what we want to achieve we cannot meditate – either we concentrate or we think about what we want to achieve. The results and insights of the formless absorptions are explained here for those who are practising them already and in order to demonstrate the abilities of the mind and how we can best use them. Indeed, the Buddha said we can step towards Enlightenment from any of the meditative absorptions.

We need to understand quite clearly that the feelings experienced in the first four meditative absorptions are quite different from those we experience in everyday life. We can experience joy in everyday life, hopefully very often, but it is not meditative joy. Similarly we can feel content in everyday life but this is not meditative contentment. Only those who practise the absorptions know the difference. However, mundane joy can also arise in meditation, for we may be joyful about the fact that we can meditate, that we try sincerely to get into it, staying with the breath or realizing an insight. But we have to bear in mind that such joy is a precondition for concentration, not concentration itself. A crucial requirement for peace and insight is the accurate recognition of what is going on within ourselves, otherwise we wouldn't learn anything from it.

The formless absorptions sometimes appear spontaneously after the fourth absorption, but they can also arise independently and although we know we have experienced something beautiful, interesting, and desirable we fail to recognize them for what they are. This is why it is so important to move along the path step by step until there is no doubt about what we experience. The Buddha clearly explained the way, so we know that the mind moves from coarse sensation, via joy and contentment, to the most subtle stillness. Such stillness does not only indicate that we have finally managed to leave all our thoughts behind, a great boon in itself, but also that we have experienced something profound.

The Fifth Meditative Absorption

With the fourth meditative absorption our mind reaches a point from which it cannot go any deeper. What happens next is an expansion that we can attain in several ways. It may appear spontaneously: from the profundity of this experience, during which the mind is entirely one-pointed, evolves a suppleness that expands the mind. Alternatively, the mind may rise from the peace of the fourth absorption and extend beyond mere awareness of the physical body (although at that time bodily form is not clearly perceived) to an experience of expansiveness. It is analogous to the first absorption, but this experience, though connected with the body, is much more refined and subtle. The mind may, if directed accordingly, go to the space taken up by our body, a space we now perceive only slightly. From here the mind goes so far beyond that an experience of infinity in limitless space ensues, the disappearance of all boundaries. The Buddha explained it in various discourses as the sense of leaving behind the trees, forests, villages, earth, moon, stars, sun, and the limits of the horizon, expanding the mind further and further. Our mind has become so pliable and malleable that it can go in any direction. Only a mind capable of that will have the ability to let go of its viewpoints entirely. The way we choose to direct our mind is no longer important; it is an experience of infinity where limits are no longer found.

From this experience we cannot but arrive at the realization that neither our own body, nor any other body, be it human, animal, tree, bush, star, or moon, was ever separate – the main emphasis being on our own body. We have an experience of infinity but nobody is there. The mind still recognizes the observer here, which is bright and clear and more intense than in the fourth absorption. The fourth absorption is peaceful and releases energy, therefore the observer is almost entirely switched off. During the experience of infinity, the observer is more active. Although there is no substantial self – and that is clear to everyone who experiences it – an observer still exists, and the mind calls it 'me'.

Not only have we left behind the idea of a substantial self, a very important step, but we also experience totality. This is the first experience of totality possible in meditation. In the fifth and sixth absorption we can understand the phrase 'we are all one' in real life. We realize very clearly that nothing is separate or has any borders – everything merges into everything else.

A mind which experiences that automatically adopts a new understanding. If we fantasize, we are not experiencing and cannot gain substantial insights. This sense of separation from other human beings, from nature, from our own thoughts and the thoughts of others, the separation between a tree, a shrub, and ourselves, relies on a deeply-ingrained wrong view. That there is no solid building-block in the whole universe has been recognized not only by our scientists. The Buddha realized it 2,500 years ago and drew his own conclusions. Scientists have determined that ultimately there are only particles of energy that come together and fall apart. In order to arrive at that conclusion we do not have to visit a laboratory. We can experience it in meditation. We have our laboratory, so to speak, within ourselves. The entire universe is contained within us and we can experience it.

Recognizing separation as a delusion helps us to adopt a new attitude in our daily interaction with people. The other person is in fact not 'other', they were also contained in that limitless space. This means that not only do our relationships with trees, flowers, rivers, and nature change, but above all there is a change in our relationship with other human beings, because it is with them that we experience most of our problems. This experience does not just lift us up from our ordinary life: it completely transforms our everyday existence.

Meditation changes our daily life. If it doesn't, we have not meditated properly – we have not paid attention or we have been dreaming. This transformation takes time and at first it happens imperceptibly. After a time, therefore, we should sit down and look back, something the Buddha strongly recommended. We can investigate, for example, what upset us perhaps two or three years ago, because today those events no longer upset us. Or we can consider how difficult it used to be for us to love someone and how easy we find it today.

In other traditions the experience of totality is often described in terms of experiencing oneself as 'all', or that all is 'me'. This is another result of the fifth and sixth absorption: 'I am all, all is me.' In some theistic religions this is regarded as heretical, but in Buddhism it is an explication of these meditative absorptions. Incidentally, the meditative absorptions used to be practised by the mystics of all religions, but they used different words to describe them. During the century of reason and in our age of technology the meditative absorptions have been pushed into the background and almost forgotten. But the human mind has a longing tendency towards them. If we wish for an experience of new levels of awareness, there is no reason why we should not be able to make it possible during intensive meditation.

Touching limitless space, then, provides us with the opportunity to feel love and compassion on a totally different basis. If we really take this step there will be concrete and palpable results. Any explanation of the meditative absorptions involves the danger that some people will think they have experienced what they have merely understood. From the first to the eighth absorption every step is a feeling. The ensuing realizations only appear after the experience of the respective absorption. The explanation is no more than an attempt to express feelings in words. On no account should we confuse thinking with feeling. Anyone can experience the absorptions, but those who are more in touch with their feelings will find it a little easier.

Love and compassion become much more accessible because we do not send out our loving-kindness, noble friendship, or readiness to help anyone, for there is no other. We are all one. Directing love towards ourselves does not make any difference either, because it means only that the heart quality has evolved and started to blossom. It is irrelevant who stands before us, even if they are pleasant or behave the way we want them to. In order to learn this, we have practised loving-kindness meditation, where we expand the feeling from close friends to an ever-widening circle. Through the experience of the fifth absorption, the feelings are no longer aimed at any particular person, because in limitless space only this feeling remains.

The Sixth Meditative Absorption
The sixth meditative absorption is analogous to the first and second. In the first subtle body or fine material absorption, where the pleasant body sensation can be felt, joy starts to rise, which then becomes the meditation object of the second absorption, through letting go the delightful physical feeling. The shift from the fifth to the sixth absorption occurs in a similar way. Limitless space, which can be perceived physically, fills with infinite consciousness, for only infinite consciousness can experience infinite space. These two arise at the same time, and in order to get from the fifth to the sixth absorption we shift our awareness from infinitude of space to infinitude of consciousness, which embraces infinite space.

We can also go out from the fifth absorption into our personal and finite consciousness and then extend it into the infinite expanse. Anyone able to sustain the experience of the fourth absorption long enough can steer their mind in this way. The greatest boon in life is a trained mind; according to the Buddha it can help us even more than our parents or our best friend.

Infinite consciousness can therefore be experienced in two ways: by expanding our consciousness into the expansiveness, or by turning from the experience of infinite space directly to the experience of infinite consciousness. In this absorption we realize that in space and consciousness there is no one.

We must be careful not to confuse the meditative absorptions with transcendental states that occur only with Stream Entry. Both space and consciousness are worldly. They are mind and body from which we are made and where everything takes place. An angry, fearful, untrained, and unaware mind is a diminished mind. It is concerned only with itself and perhaps a few people close by. It cannot let go of the ego-illusion because it is constantly occupied with the ego. However, a mind that is purified by concentration and mindfulness can detach itself from the limitations we impose on ourselves and which so often get us into trouble. The dilemma of the limited mind is solved by a mind working towards concentration. It purifies itself in everyday existence further and further and can then expand into infinity.

This expansion clearly shows the mind that although it exists, it does not belong to 'me'. Here we can realize quite strikingly that the observer disappears into infinity. He is here, and he does observe, but he is also infinite. Once we have got to know ourselves as limited body and limited mind, and the observer has become infinite, we again face the same question: who is this 'me'? This is the central question of the Buddha's teaching.

With the help of the sixth absorption we can recognize more clearly that there is indeed consciousness, but there is no one who owns it. If the mind is sufficiently purified through its preliminary efforts it will find much relief from these insights. This relief is but an inkling of how it can be once we really let go of the ego, so for most people these two absorptions add momentum and urgency to their desire for liberation.

Of course, if 'I' want to be liberated, it won't work. The same block appears if I want to get rid of 'my' dukkha. Dukkha and liberation exist, but the ego forms a barrier between them. If we want to reach freedom – and the first step towards it, Stream Entry, which confers only a very limited degree of freedom, the kindergarten of Enlightenment so to speak – we need to find out who is in the way of Enlightenment, not who wants to get it.

These two meditative absorptions give us a taste of how things are when there is no one in the way. Their limitlessness is not the same as complete dissolution, but it points towards the eventual dissolution of our limitations. That again is something we cannot concoct with our minds, but only experience.

At the same time we find an entirely new basis for love and compassion. Far from our ingrained attitude which distinguishes between amiable people and less agreeable ones, we arrive at the experience that love and compassion are the only emotions in this infinity. Every one of us is contained in this infinite space and consciousness, but no one can be located. All negating, rejecting, disliking is harmful to all people in our realm. All love and compassion helps. Hence we recognize through the absorptions that any other emotion is pointless and unskilful, just spoiling infinity. This is a much greater folly than polluting our environment. Once we have experienced and understood all that, we gain new access to our feelings. This doorway is always open to us if we have sufficiently practised the absorptions.

The Seventh Meditative Absorption

In the seventh absorption, which follows on from the previous absorptions, the mind realizes that in infinite space and in infinite consciousness there is absolutely nothing to be found. At that time the awareness is directed towards the experience, which can sometimes appear as flickering movement. The mind takes in through the seventh absorption that there is nothing to which it can attach itself. In the meantime, the mind has become so subtle that it no longer needs anything to which to attach itself.

A mind that never meditates is attached to its opinions and to all it sees, hears, smells, tastes, and touches. A mind somewhat polished through meditation doubts that what it thinks is really true, and whether it really already knows everything. Even more refinement lets it regard its opinions as just opinions, until it stops taking on any opinions whatsoever. This is a pointer to the path to nibbāna, how we start to know the possibility of one day letting go and totally losing oneself. This, however, includes the entire path of the meditative absorptions and the resulting insights, towards which we can work with the help of concentration. Our will needs to be so purified that it is no longer affected by our wanting or not wanting, or by our opinions, but is free to step out into the universe. A mind that continues to cling to its desires cannot yet bear this infinity.

The way has to be walked slowly, step by step. We cannot omit a step, even though we might tell ourselves we are one step further than we really are. It is the way it is, at whichever point we are. The Buddha compared this path of practice to the ocean: we wade slowly in from the beach, getting wet little by little, until we are completely submerged.

The Eighth Meditative Absorption

The seventh meditative absorption is the third of the insight absorptions and leaves behind such a strong impression that the mind knows and feels that this infinity does not contain anything on to which we can hold. As infinity encompasses us, the mind is ready to lose the ego and merge with the primeval source of being where no ego can be found.

The seventh meditative absorption leads to the eighth, which is analogous to the fourth. In the fourth absorption the mind rests, while the observer is still active in the background, but in the eighth absorption, the mind is no longer as awake and cognizant, instead, it rests within itself. This feeling is difficult to explain. It is a leaving behind of the four mental groups of existence (*khandhas*). The eighth absorption is also called neither-perception-nor-non-perception. Perception is the third step after sense contact and feeling, and is our observer. During the eighth absorption the observer is so minimal that it cannot say anything about the experience. The mind, however, dwells in utter peace and receives an enormous amount of energy. It shows us how much dukkha there is in thought and observation, even while we think up the most lovely fantasies. The result of the eighth meditative absorption is that we recognize the continuous mental activity as dukkha. A body that has to work as hard as we constantly demand from our mind cannot endure it. Only a meditator can create some peace for the mind, in the absorptions.

After the eighth absorption it becomes especially clear how burdensome for us is thought. A human being is therefore always afflicted by dukkha because every sense contact leads to thought. The Buddha entirely approved of flight from dukkha into the meditative absorptions. Similarly, we can enjoy sensual pleasures if we stop searching for them and just experience them as they occur. If we saw only the dukkha that will befall us when we emerge from the eighth absorption, we would get so depressed that we would no longer pursue the path. By recognizing dukkha, however, we can find sufficient zest and energy to enable us to let go of ego-illusion.

Avalokiteśvara, the Bodhisattva, was immersed in the deepest wisdom. Absorbed in the deepest wisdom, he recognized that everything in the world is empty, and all bitterness and suffering he erased by saying:

'Śāriputra, the world of form is nothing but emptiness and emptiness is nothing but the world of form. This means form is identical with emptiness, and emptiness is identical with form. The same is true for feelings, thoughts, volition, and knowledge.

'Śāriputra, all things in reality are empty. Nothing arises and nothing ceases to be. Nothing is impure and nothing is purified. Nothing increases, nothing decreases.

'In emptiness there is no body, no feeling, no thought, no will, no consciousness. There are no eyes, ears, nose, tongue, body, or mind. There is no sight, sound, smell, taste, touch, or thought; nor is there ignorance or knowledge. There is no growing old, no death, nor end of them. There is no suffering, and no arising of suffering, no extinction, and no way to liberation. There is no wisdom, and no attainment of insight either. And because the Bodhisattva dwells in this wisdom, his mind is untroubled and free from fear. He is free from all delusions, dreams, and projections, and experiences present nirvāṇa.

'All Enlightened Ones of all times – past, present, and future – follow the way of perfect wisdom and thus attain the great liberation. All walk this path of perfect wisdom and thus attain the great liberation.

'Therefore let us experience the deepest wisdom, all of us together. This is the great mantra, the great word of truth, of matchless profundity, which allays all suffering; hear the impeccable truth, unfolding ultimate wisdom.

Come, all of you, come all, to the great liberation, to the great, infinite liberation, to Enlightenment. This is the heart of perfect wisdom.'

Gate, gate, pāragate, pārasaṁgate, bodhi, svāhā.

Hṛdaya Prajñāpāramitā Sūtra

The Heart of Perfect Wisdom

THE HṚDAYA PRAJÑĀPĀRAMITĀ SŪTRA is a well known text, especially cherished in the Korean and Japanese Zen traditions, and is
about a thousand years old. Its title is Sanskrit: *Hṛdaya* means heart,
prajñā is wisdom, *pāramitā* virtue, and a *sūtra* is a discourse (*hadaya*,
paññā, *pāramī*, and *sutta* are the corresponding terms in Pāli, but we
will use Sanskrit terms here because we are discussing a Sanskrit
text). It could be literally translated 'Discourse on the Virtue of
Wisdom'. Usually, however, it is translated 'Heart of Perfect Wisdom'
or simply 'Heart Sūtra'.

It was composed by a great Zen master, and explains in brief the
final elements in the chain of transcendental dependent arising,
starting with freedom from negative emotion, and progressing up to
full Enlightenment. Though it can only be understood from the point
of view of absolute truth, and our ordinary intellect cannot relate to
it, it is a popular discourse and frequently quoted. It begins as
follows:

> *Avalokiteśvara, the Bodhisattva, was immersed in the*
> *deepest wisdom.*

Avalokiteśvara comes from the pantheon of divine figures that origi-
nated in India at about the same time the Buddha's teaching was
being disseminated through the subcontinent. He is often depicted
with many arms, symbolizing his transcendental willingness and
ability to accomplish the good and look after countless beings, and

he therefore represents compassion in its male form. Kwan Yin is a female form of the same figure in the Chinese tradition.

A *Bodhisattva* (Pāli: *Bodhisatta*) is someone totally committed to the search for Enlightenment. The Buddha was therefore a Bodhisattva before he became the Buddha. *Bodhi* means 'Enlightenment' and *sattva* means 'being', so the term is literally 'Enlightenment being', but it can be said to denote 'the one who is searching for Enlightenment and is dedicated to working towards that goal.'

> *Absorbed in the deepest wisdom, he recognized that*
> *everything in the world is empty.*

Here we have the Bodhisattva Avalokiteśvara absorbed in deepest contemplation and recognizing that everything we experience in the world, whether in terms of the body, or in terms of feeling, or perception, or thought, or consciousness, is in reality empty. The five categories mentioned here are the five *skandhas* (*khandhas* in Pāli), usually translated as 'groups of existence' or 'aggregates', and they distinguish what our experience comprises. In illustrations of the cyclic chain of mundane dependent arising a demon, draped in a tiger-skin, holds a wheel symbolizing this cycle, and he wears a diadem of five skulls, representing the *skandhas*.

Above all, these five components out of which human beings are made – body, feeling, perception, thought, and sense consciousness – are empty, or void. But what are they devoid of? They are devoid of substance. That is, they are devoid of anything that could give them any meaning. We can get into enormous difficulty here, trying to understand this notion. Indeed, there is the possibility of a quite catastrophic misunderstanding. Emptiness does not mean these things do not exist in the world – without doubt the world in all its diversity does exist. But everything in it is characterized by impermanence. There is nothing whatsoever that can be found to stand as an exception to this rule, which may also be expressed as the governing principle that nothing exists in itself. Thus the things that seem to us to be solid are in reality merely appearances, because they are constantly passing away. There is nothing in them that can be preserved or possessed. So it is in this sense that they are empty.

And all bitterness and suffering he erased by saying,
'Śāriputra, the world of form is nothing but emptiness and
emptiness is nothing but the world of form.'

Abolishing all bitterness and suffering means bringing all *duḥkha* (Pāli: *dukkha*) to an end. Śāriputra was the historical Buddha's right-hand man and the disciple with greatest wisdom, so people who wanted to express their Enlightenment would go to see either the Buddha or Śāriputra. And this is what Avalokiteśvara does here. Avalokiteśvara realizes the complete cessation of all bitterness and suffering within him, having experienced reality itself. He realizes that the world of form is empty and that emptiness is nothing but the world of form. Emptiness means lack of substance, that there is no fundamental core to anything; humans as well as animals, to-gether with the entire natural world, indeed all material objects, hold nothing fixed or substantial within them. The simple truth he has realized is that emptiness pertains to everything. Yet without actual personal experience of what the term refers to it is difficult to understand. Another way to put it is to say that nothing is all and all is nothing – but these words are also difficult to understand.

The world of form is empty – it contains nothing – and this reality extends throughout everything. It is we ourselves who create the duality of our world in discriminating between things and saying, 'Here is a human being. Here is a flower. Here is an animal. Here is something good and there is something bad.' With such discrimina-tion the whole merry-go-round of our thoughts begins, from which we do not escape because we are constantly finding something new to judge.

Above all, of course, we judge ourselves: 'I have done well here,' 'I have failed there,' 'I would like to do this better,' 'I have done that already,' 'I am very good,' 'I am bad.' This inclination to distinguish and evaluate, to pick and choose, makes it impossible for us to recognize that in all the objects of our estimations and judgements there is nothing, that this nothing encompasses everything, and that there is no duality whatsoever. It only appears to be the case that everything is different and separate. This world of ours is one of illusion, called *māyā* in the Indian tradition. But because our eyes see things and our ears hear things we believe in this illusion and take it for real.

> *This means form is identical with emptiness, and emptiness is identical with form.*

There are no things in themselves; there are only appearances. What appears before us as real is in truth like foam on the surface of the ocean. The little bubbles of foam completely forget they are in no way separate from the ocean upon which they appear so briefly, and they start getting all sorts of ideas about themselves, saying to one another, 'You know, I am a much nicer bubble than you,' or 'I am quite tall, and you are so small,' or 'I am rather more intelligent than you are,' or 'Look at me – I can do a double somersault.'

These ideas do not alter the fact that in reality these bubbles are nothing but the ocean, that they have been formed by the movement of the ocean. What we identify as the forms of individual things are one with emptiness, as bubbles are one with the ocean and the ocean is one with the bubbles – they all partake of the one unity.

> *The same is true for feelings, thoughts, volition, and knowledge.*

Again, Avalokiteśvara brings in the five *skandhas* (and it is sometimes worth taking a slightly different view of them, as in this translation. What is usually 'perception' is here translated 'thought', and instead of 'consciousness' we have here 'knowledge'). He explains to Śāriputra that if there is nothing in us beyond these five elements, they are themselves also empty. Just as our own claim to be more than the sum of these elements is apparent rather than real, so they themselves are only appearances, with no stable identity, however much importance we invest in what they add up to. Then he repeats himself:

> *Śāriputra, all things in reality are empty.*

Up to this point what we seem to have is an elucidation of the kind of insight I would call a 'path moment' – a single moment with nothing arising and nothing ceasing. Before attaining this insight and describing it, Avalokiteśvara has had to work towards it by finding a completely new orientation of consciousness. But now we

THE HEART OF PERFECT WISDOM 183

hear about the fruits that Avalokiteśvara enjoys, as he explicates the vision of absolute reality that arises subsequent to his insight.

In the writings of Nāgārjuna, one of the great Mahāyāna teachers, we read that the Dharma (the Sanskrit equivalent of the Pāli *Dhamma*) cannot be understood unless we are able to distinguish between absolute and relative truth. The path by which we make our way in the world is of course that of relative truth, where we perceive everything in dualistic terms and all appearances have a meaning. But there is another path we may take which is that of absolute reality, where appearances are no longer appearances, and reality is seen as emptiness. This absolute reality, *nibbāna* in Pāli, is better-known by the Sanskrit term *nirvāṇa*.

Nothing arises and nothing ceases to be. Nothing is impure and nothing is purified. Nothing increases, nothing decreases.

In absolute reality there is no arising and no decaying; it is the deathless and therefore the birthless. All the world of appearances that we hold to be so important has been absorbed back into the reality out of which it arose. Like little bubbles of spindrift on the ocean of absolute reality, having recognized this absolute reality we have allowed ourselves to be absorbed back into the ocean. We no longer want to be little bubbles bobbing about and asserting our own special bubblehood, having realized that such self-assertion brings only duḥkha. And through this insight, and thus our absorption back into the primordial ground of being, it is seen that nothing arises or ceases. Nothing can be born there or die, nothing can increase or decrease. There is no duality, there are no opposites, no separation. It is a totality, without the appearance of divisible phenomena. The illusory world is restored to emptiness.

In emptiness there is no body, no feeling, no thought, no will, no consciousness.

In this emptiness the categories of the five skandhas do not arise; nor, therefore, does human existence.

There are no eyes, ears, nose, tongue, body, or mind.

If there are no skandhas, whether of the body or the mind, there are no sense contacts either. So this takes us the opposite way from the mundane chain of dependent arising, in which the arising of body and mind is shown to lead to sense contacts. Here, having realized how sense contacts arise from the skandhas, one is further able to realize that in reality the skandhas are themselves all illusory and void, so that there are no longer any conditions for the appearance of body and mind. Without sense organs there can, of course, be no sense contact, thus

There is no sight, sound, smell, taste, touch, or thought; nor is there ignorance or knowledge.

Ignorance, which stands as the main driving force of the worldly chain of dependent arising and therefore of all existence, is no longer there either. There is no one to *be* ignorant.

Of course, this account is not describing the exact nature of absolute reality. All any description can do is point towards such an insight. It can never communicate its true meaning to those who have not had the experience. What it can do is convey how all duḥkha comes to an end. It is impossible to eradicate suffering in the world, but it is certainly possible to eradicate the ego, and therefore to let go of duality. Then we will no longer be able to take for reality the ultimately illusory distinctions that we draw. We recognize the five skandhas, in which our existence aggregates or amasses together, as also illusory, and no longer regard that resultant existence as absolutely important. At the moment of such realization we understand that the same must go for everything whatsoever, and that we should never feel the need to lose contact with this primordial ground of being, for whenever we do so we shall find only duḥkha.

There is no growing old, no death, nor end of them.

Ageing and death do not occur there, because there is no birth. Rendered into our image of the ocean this means that if there are no bubbles on this ocean, they won't have to burst; if a bubble is not born it will not need to die. Indeed, the duḥkha of ageing and death ceases when – and only when – there is no possibility of birth. There is no other way to avoid this duḥkha.

There is no suffering, and no arising of suffering, no extinction, and no way to liberation.

The recognition of duḥkha has to come first – an irresistible recognition of duḥkha so strong that attachment to body and mind dissolves. Completely letting go of attachment to oneself, an attachment that must always draw suffering in its wake, opens the door that leads to the end of all suffering. One may then be able to cognize one's own self as only apparently a separate and individual entity, and no particular importance can be attached to a self that is seen as such a delusive phenomenon.

We are then prepared to let it be absorbed back into the primordial ground of being, where there is no longer the possibility of self-cognition, or of non-cognition of the self, of birth, of death, of sight, sound, smell, taste. Also, there is no longer any suffering or the cessation of suffering, they too are found to be empty. Where there is nothing – where we understand that in reality there is nothing from the beginning – nothing can be suffered, and where nothing is suffered, suffering need not be overcome.

The world of appearances deceives us into believing that it can satisfy us, for our minds are very quick to forget about the unpleasant side of things and to dwell only upon the pleasurable aspects. We could call the mind a magician: it can conjure up anything, but it can also direct itself towards awareness of absolute truth.

We find the same kind of experience described in all mystical writings, and from all types of mystics. Although the way of expression differs, the kind of experience pointed to often seems the same. For example, Meister Eckhart, the German late-medieval Dominican friar, said, 'Man is a nothing' – and was promptly accused of heresy.

Because the world we live in brings suffering, we search for freedom from suffering. We may experience such freedom momentarily, but it is always impermanent – as impermanent as every moment of suffering. Everything is continuously perishing. Therefore, in reality, nothing is ever actually there; it slips through our fingers as we look at it.

On a clock we can observe this process taking place. Every moment is a move towards the next moment. If it stands still, the whole process of which the moment is a part is broken. The nature of time is that it passes, and our experience can be neither of the future nor of the past. What, then, remains? Only the fraction of a second in the perception of a flicker of the second hand – which is perhaps as good an image as any to convey the fact that there *is* nothing. The past is gone, the future is not yet present. Only the hand moves; everything else is fiction.

As there is no suffering, there is no cessation either, nor is there a way to liberation. Avalokiteśvara has walked the path of liberation already. It only exists in the world and is obsolete once the world has been seen through. On the absolute level nothing at all happens, there is utter stillness. Nor is there anyone to enjoy it.

There is no wisdom, and no attainment of insight either.

Ignorance and wisdom exist together in our familiar world of appearances. In this world there are foolish and clever people, people who go the way of wisdom and seek the way to liberation, and people who are not interested in all that. Yet as soon as we travel on the path of the absolute, these distinctions are gone. In the primordial ground of being there is nothing to know or not to know, no searching and no finding.

Even the term 'primordial ground of being' must be dropped before we can understand what it refers to. It is just a term. All terms necessarily refer to relative reality, even the term 'absolute reality'. We are faced with the problem of having to express supramundane experience in terms that can only be used to express mundane experience. This is why the expressions used are so often paradoxical and impossible to understand.

And because the Bodhisattva dwells in this wisdom, his mind is untroubled and free from fear.

Whoever attains this realization during their lifetime has an entirely untroubled mind. They no longer feel affected by what the bubbles do, for they now know that in reality these bubbles consist only of air and that they break up when their bodies are old. This realization lifts the burden from the mind, leaving it untroubled and without fear.

So what is it to be fearless? It is no longer to have an ego to be protected, status and dignity to be asserted, or an insight to be proven. In this way no place for attack is offered, thus no need to fear anything arises. The body is no longer a personal possession. The mind, too, is unowned. Both are phenomena of a world of appearances, coming together only to disintegrate again in the moment of death. In the moment of complete Enlightenment, all fear, including the fear of that moment of death, is dispelled.

All unenlightened beings are subject to fear, even through the first three stages of Enlightenment, when there are still some traces of ego. Fear takes various shapes and names in our minds: fear of the dark, fear of other people, fear of old age, fear of illness, fear of terrorism and warfare. In our world of appearances we have constantly to give names to everything to embody it in form. We limit everything within space and time, just so that we can grasp and comprehend it.

Behind all fear lies the fear of the ego coming under attack or being annihilated, whether physically, emotionally, or mentally. As long as there is an ego there will be fear. The stronger the egocentricity, the greater the fear, and the more unpleasant one's experience of life. Freedom from fear comes only at the point of liberation, with the realization of emptiness.

He is free from all delusions, dreams, and projections, and experiences present nirvāṇa.

We dream up ideas about how nirvāṇa might be. We develop fantasies about how we might arrange a fabulous life for ourselves. We have particular ideas of ourselves and other people, and we imagine heaven or paradise and think of angels. But all these fancies are simply unfounded – a dreaming sleep that is broken only upon transcendental realization. All things are just apparitions, coming and going, one endlessly following the other. If we think how many people have already lived on this little planet, how they have come and gone, and that now it's our turn – and if we think how we are here for a moment before we too pass on and make way for others to follow, and that no one, in the end, will remember us as we truly were – we will see that we are part of a world of phantasmagoria, of make-believe.

Realization is pure – empty of all imagining: 'Nothing is all, and all is nothing.' This is the end of all dreams. We can experience nirvāṇa now, during our own life; we can live this freedom. The Buddha was Enlightened by the age of thirty-five, and continued to live until he was eighty, in a state of total liberation, using his endowment to help others escape their own make-believe world, in the knowledge that he could help those with 'but little dust on their eyes'.

> *All Enlightened Ones of all times – past, present, and future – follow the way of perfect wisdom and thus attain the great liberation.*

'Buddha' is not a name, but a title, meaning 'Enlightened One', and there have been Buddhas before. The Buddha called Siddhārtha Gautama, of whose teaching we are able to avail ourselves, is the seventh Buddha of this world cycle according to Theravādin tradition (the twenty-fourth according to Mahāyāna tradition). All these Buddhas, one after another, rediscover the same way. Indeed, all Enlightened Ones go by the same path and arrive at the same realization of absolute truth.

The Buddha of the present time is the one to whose teaching we refer today. The next Buddha is said to be one who will be called Maitreya (Metteyya in Pāli), but his time lies far ahead, so we should not count on living at the time of a Buddha, as such times are very rare. We are better advised to embark on our great task right now, and make best use of the present conditions rather than hold out hope for more favourable ones in future. Enlightenment is possible not only when a Buddha is alive, but at any time when the Dharma – the instructions he leaves behind him to guide us in the right direction – is alive. It is still alive as long as we can discover it by reading it and hearing it today.

> *All walk on this path of perfect wisdom and thus attain the great liberation.*

Having said all this, Avalokiteśvara goes on to encourage others to experience this wisdom for themselves:

> *Therefore let us experience the deepest wisdom, all of us together. This is the great mantra, the great word of truth, of*

*matchless profundity, which allays all suffering; hear the
impeccable truth, unfolding ultimate wisdom.*

At this point a verse follows, like a spell:

*Come, all of you, come all, to the great liberation, to the
great, infinite liberation, to Enlightenment. This is the heart
of perfect wisdom.*

A mantra then follows in Sanskrit:

Gate, gate, pāragate, pārasaṁgate, bodhi, svāhā.

which literally translated means:

*Go, go,
Go beyond,
Go beyond yourself,
Blessed Enlightenment.*

With these words the Bodhisattava Avalokiteśvara addresses all
beings; they are all to join in going 'to the great freedom, to the great,
infinite freedom, to Enlightenment, to the heart of perfect wisdom.'
    The title, *Hṛdaya Prajñāpāramitā* or 'the heart of perfect wisdom', is
well chosen, for it suggests the accomplishment of wisdom to be the
liberation of the heart. Wisdom is a realization, but it is also a feeling,
so the heart has to be involved. If we understand the text's formula-
tions intellectually, and this is difficult enough, its insights remain
alien and mysterious until we can experience them in our heart. Only
by means of this dual faculty of head and heart do we open up to a
freedom from all duality, from all imaginings, from all separation.
And also from all trouble, for once the emptiness, the being nothing,
has been acknowledged and dwelt within, nothing can ever again
afford us trouble in any way whatsoever. All fear is gone, for the way
is travelled. Whoever has trodden this path has said to the Buddha
or to Śāriputra, 'The path is travelled, the work is done, there is no
more to do.'
    When this feeling that nothing more has to be done unfolds, true
peace and true stillness have been attained. This is not physical

stillness, but an inner life of peace and calm; it is here that all the work is done. This conclusion constitutes the whole purpose and point of meditation. If we do not regard meditation and the path in this light, we will get stuck and make little if any progress in our meditation. On the other hand, if we make a real effort in our meditation, if we truly commit ourselves to the path, we will inevitably get there. A deep investigation of the mind will show us that our innermost wish is to experience profound peace, contentment, and happiness, in the cessation of all hankering – and only on the path can we achieve this.

The *Hṛdaya Prajñāpāramitā Sūtra* is not the word of the Buddha, but the Buddha expressed the same experience and insight in the following words:

> There is such a sphere without earth or water, without fire or air
> [the four basic 'elements' from which all matter is constituted].
> Neither the sphere of infinite space is there, nor the sphere of
> limitless consciousness [the fifth and sixth meditative absorptions],
> neither the sphere of no-thing, nor the sphere of which one can
> hardly speak any more in terms of perception [the seventh and
> eighth absorptions]. Neither this world is there, nor the other world,
> neither sun nor moon. Neither coming is there, nor going, nor
> permanence, neither birth nor death. Nirvāṇa is based on nothing,
> unmoved, beyond all imagination. It is the end of suffering.*

Nirvāṇa is beyond what we can imagine; it cannot be thought. We have therefore to give up thinking and in doing so to be ready to give up ourselves. Then it will be possible to experience this truth in which there is neither birth nor death, neither coming nor going. This is the end of all suffering.

---

* Udāna viii.1

BIBLIOGRAPHY

The quotations given in this book are our own translations from the German. Other English translations of the texts quoted include the following:

Sangharakshita (trans.), *Dhammapada*, Windhorse Publications, Birmingham 2001

Thomas Cleary (trans.), *The Dhammapada*, Bantam, New York 1995

John Ross Carter and Mahinda Palihawadana (trans.), *The Dhammapada*, Oxford University Press, Oxford 2000

H. Saddhatissa (trans.), *The Sutta-Nipāta*, Curzon, Richmond 1994

F. L. Woodward and E.M. Hare (trans.), *The Book of the Gradual Sayings (Aṅguttara-Nikāya)*, Pali Text Society, London (five volumes: 1932, -33, -34, -35, -36)

T.W. Rhys Davids (trans.), *The Questions of King Milinda*, Motilal Banarsidass, Delhi (1997 reprint of Oxford University Press 1890 edition, two volumes)

Edward Conze (trans. and commentary), *Buddhist Wisdom: The Diamond Sutra and the Heart Sūtra*, Vintage, New York 2001

Bhikkhu Ñāṇamoli (trans.), *The Path of Purification (Visuddhimagga)*, Buddhist Publication Society, Kandy 1991

Peter Masefield (trans.), *The Udāna*, Pali Text Society, Oxford 1997

John D. Ireland (trans.), *The Udāna and the Itivuttaka*, Buddhist Publication Society, Kandy 1997

INDEX

The windhorse symbolizes the energy of the Enlightened mind carrying the truth of the Buddha's teachings to all corners of the world. On its back the windhorse bears three jewels: a brilliant gold jewel represents the Buddha, the ideal of Enlightenment, a sparkling blue jewel represents the teachings of the Buddha, the Dharma, and a glowing red jewel, the community of the Buddha's enlightened followers, the Sangha. Windhorse Publications, through the medium of books, similarly takes these three jewels out to the world.

Windhorse Publications is a Buddhist publishing house, staffed by practising Buddhists. We place great emphasis on producing books of high quality, accessible and relevant to those interested in Buddhism at whatever level. Drawing on the whole range of the Buddhist tradition, Windhorse books include translations of traditional texts, commentaries, books that make links with Western culture and ways of life, biographies of Buddhists, and manuals on meditation.

As a charitable institution we welcome donations to help us continue our work. We also welcome manuscripts on aspects of Buddhism or meditation. For orders and catalogues contact

WINDHORSE PUBLICATIONS	WINDHORSE BOOKS	WEATHERHILL INC
11 PARK ROAD	P O BOX 574	41 MONROE TURNPIKE
BIRMINGHAM	NEWTOWN	TRUMBULL
B13 8AB	NSW 2042	CT 06611
UK	AUSTRALIA	USA

Windhorse Publications is an arm of the Friends of the Western Buddhist Order, which has more than sixty centres on five continents. Through these centres, members of the Western Buddhist Order offer regular programmes of events for the general public and for more experienced students. These include meditation classes, public talks, study on Buddhist themes and texts, and 'bodywork' classes such as t'ai chi, yoga, and massage. The FWBO also runs several retreat centres and the Karuna Trust, a fund-raising charity that supports social welfare projects in the slums and villages of India.

Many FWBO centres have residential spiritual communities and ethical businesses associated with them. Arts activities are encouraged too, as is the development of strong bonds of friendship between people who share the same ideals. In this way the FWBO is developing a unique approach to Buddhism, not simply as a set of techniques, less still as an exotic cultural interest, but as a creatively directed way of life for people living in the modern world.

If you would like more information about the FWBO please visit www.fwbo.org or write to

LONDON BUDDHIST CENTRE	ARYALOKA
51 ROMAN ROAD	HEARTWOOD CIRCLE
LONDON	NEWMARKET
E2 0HU	NH 03857
UK	USA

ALSO FROM WINDHORSE

KALYANAVACA (editor)

THE MOON AND FLOWERS: A WOMAN'S PATH TO ENLIGHTENMENT

This book brings together essays by nineteen women who have been ordained within the Buddhist tradition. They come from different countries and have very different lifestyles. Their firm commitment to Buddhism is perhaps the only thing they all have in common.

Here they demonstrate how they are trying to bring the various aspects and concerns of their daily lives into harmony with their Buddhist ideals and practice. They talk about feminism, motherhood, work, sexuality, friendship, and many other issues. The wide variety of personal experience woven together with key principles and practices makes for a vivid and richly textured portrait of what it means to follow the Buddhist path as a woman in the modern world.

304 pages, with photographs
ISBN 0 904766 89 6
£11.99/$23.95

SANGHARAKSHITA

DHAMMAPADA: THE WAY OF TRUTH

The *Dhammapada* is one of the most popular and influential of Buddhist scriptures. The universality of its message, the depth of its teaching, and the refined simplicity of its language have earned it an honoured place in world literature.

It can be taken as a straightforward and practical summary of the essential teachings of the Buddha, but – much more than that – the *Dhammapada* is a poetic representation of a sublime spiritual ideal.

164 pages
ISBN 1 899579 35 4
£9.99/$19.95